DRAMA CLASSICS

The Drama Classics series a[...] [...] plays in affordable paperback editions for students, actors and theatregoers. The hallmarks of the series are accessible introductions, uncluttered texts and an overall theatrical perspective.

Given that readers may be encountering a particular play for the first time, the introduction seeks to fill in the theatrical/historical background and to outline the chief themes rather than concentrate on interpretational and textual analysis. Similarly the play-texts themselves are free of footnotes and other interpolations: instead there is an end-glossary of 'difficult' words and phrases.

The texts of the English-language plays in the series have been prepared taking full account of all existing scholarship. The foreign-language plays have been newly translated into a modern English that is both actable and accurate: many of the translators regularly have their work staged professionally.

Edited until his early death by Kenneth McLeish, the Drama Classics series continues with his aim of providing a first-class library of dramatic literature representing the best of world theatre.

Associate editors:
Professor Trevor R. Griffiths
Visiting Professor in Humanities, University of Hertfordshire
Dr Colin Counsell
School of Humanities, Arts and Languages,
London Metropolitan University

DRAMA CLASSICS *the first hundred*

The Alchemist
All for Love
Andromache
Antigone
Arden of Faversham
Bacchae
Bartholomew Fair
The Beaux Stratagem
The Beggar's Opera
Birds
Celestina
The Changeling
A Chaste Maid in
  Cheapside
The Cherry Orchard
Children of the Sun
El Cid
The Country Wife
The Dance of Death
The Devil is an Ass
Doctor Faustus
A Doll's House
Don Juan
The Duchess of
  Malfi
Edward II
Electra (Euripides)
Electra (Sophocles)
An Enemy of the
  People
Every Man in his
  Humour
Everyman
Faust
A Flea in her Ear
Frogs
Fuenteovejuna
The Game of Love
  and Chance
Ghosts
The Government
  Inspector

Hecuba
Hedda Gabler
The Hypochondriac
The Importance of
  Being Earnest
An Ideal Husband
An Italian Straw Hat
The Jew of Malta
The Knight of the
  Burning Pestle
The Lady from the Sea
The Learned Ladies
Lady Windermere's
  Fan
Life is a Dream
The Lower Depths
The Lucky Chance
Lulu
Lysistrata
The Magistrate
The Malcontent
The Man of Mode
The Marriage of
  Figaro
Mary Stuart
The Master Builder
Medea
The Misanthrope
The Miser
Miss Julie
A Month in the
  Country
A New Way to Pay
  Old Debts
Oedipus
The Oresteia
Peer Gynt
Phedra
The Playboy of the
  Western World
The Recruiting
  Officer

The Revenger's
  Tragedy
The Rivals
The Roaring Girl
La Ronde
Rosmersholm
The Rover
Scapino
The School for
  Scandal
The Seagull
The Servant of Two
  Masters
She Stoops to Conquer
The Shoemakers'
  Holiday
Six Characters in Search
  of an Author
The Spanish Tragedy
Spring's Awakening
Summerfolk
Tartuffe
Three Sisters
'Tis Pity She's a
  Whore
Too Clever by Half
Ubu
Uncle Vanya
Volpone
The Way of the
  World
The White Devil
The Wild Duck
A Woman of No
  Importance
Women Beware
  Women
Women of Troy
Woyzeck

*The publishers welcome
suggestions for further titles*

DRAMA CLASSICS

KING OEDIPUS

and

OEDIPUS AT KOLONOS

by

Sophocles

translated and introduced by
Kenneth McLeish

NICK HERN BOOKS

London

www.nickhernbooks.co.uk

A Drama Classic

King Oedipus and *Oedipus at Kolonos* first published in Great Britain in this translation as a paperback original in 2001 by Nick Hern Books Ltd, 14 Larden Road, London W3 7ST.

Reprinted 2007

Copyright in the Introduction © 2001 by Nick Hern Books Ltd

Copyright in this translation from the Ancient Greek © 2001 by the Estate of the late Kenneth McLeish

Kenneth McLeish died in 1997. The text has been edited, and the introduction completed, by Michael Sargent

Typeset by Country Setting, Kingsdown, Kent CT14 8ES
Printed by CPI Bookmarque, Croydon, CR0 4TD

A CIP catalogue record for this book is available from the British Library

ISBN 978 1 85459 610 9

Introduction

Sophocles (c 496-406 BC)

Sophocles was well-to-do (the son of an arms-manufacturer) and he had a distinguished career in public life. He was a confidant of politicians, most notably of Pericles, the great statesman of Athens' period of glory in the mid-fifth century BC. He served as a general and as overseer of public funds, and his lifelong interest in public health led him to sponsor the building of a healing temple dedicated to the god Asklepios – work for which he was given the posthumous honour of being declared a national hero, under the name Dexion (the 'Receiver').

From his youth Sophocles was renowned as musician and dancer. He made his first public appearance as one of a group of boy musicians celebrating the Greek victory over the Persians at Salamis (480 BC), and his first dramatic successes were as author and musician/actor, taking the parts of a lyre-player who challenged the gods, and of the princess Nausicaa, in a story based on Homer's *Odyssey*. He wrote some 123 plays altogether and won prizes with 96 of them. Legend says that his son Iophon, also a dramatist, took him to court in 406 BC, claiming he was too senile to manage his own affairs – and the aged dramatist triumphantly defended himself by declaiming a chorus from the play he was currently writing, *Oedipus at Kolonos*.

Like all Greek playwrights Sophocles not only wrote the words but composed the music (perhaps a particular interest of his) and played the leading roles in his own plays. There is a story that he gave up acting in mid-career because of voice-strain; but it is equally plausible that his busy life simply left him no time for it. Seven complete plays survive. The earliest is *Ajax* (performed when he was in his forties); apart from *Ajax* and *Antigone* (dating perhaps from 442 BC) all are thought to have been written in the last three decades of his long life.

In his own time, Sophocles was famous for the gentleness and serenity of his character. In his work, he was a controlled, technical writer, compared with the surging inspiration of Aeschylus or the experimentation of Euripides. Aristotle admired him most of all the ancient tragedians, and credits him with technical innovations – increasing the number of the Chorus from 12 to 15, and introducing painted scenery and the use of three actors instead of two. This radically moved Greek tragedy away from ritual and towards drama based on situations and character; there are notable scenes involving three actors in both the Oedipus plays. Sophocles' choruses are some of the most limpid and technically assured of all surviving Greek poetry.

King Oedipus: **What Happens in the Play**

As the play opens, Oedipus addresses a group of Theban citizens outside his palace gates. They have come to beg him to find some end for the plague which is destroying the city. He says that he has sent Kreon ('His Honour') to Delphi to ask advice of the oracle, and that whatever

Apollo orders, he will do it. Kreon returns and announces Apollo's words. The plague is caused by a murderer in Thebes, who killed Laios, the former king, and lives on unpunished. He must be found and dealt with, or the city will die. Oedipus promises to act, and the Chorus sing and dance in honour of Apollo.

Oedipus lays a formal curse on the murderer and all who shelter him. He says he will find him, will fight for Laios as if for his own father. He asks Teiresias, the blind prophet, for information. At first Teiresias is reluctant to speak, but when Oedipus insists, he names the murderer – Oedipus himself. Oedipus accuses Teiresias of plotting subversion with Kreon; Teiresias offers Oedipus more riddling information about his own parentage and that of his children. He goes, and the Chorus sing agitatedly, asking the gods to settle the matter and end the doubt that racks them.

Kreon comes on, bewildered by Oedipus' accusation that he is trying to steal the throne. He and Oedipus quarrel violently, and even Jokasta is unable to calm them. After Kreon leaves, she asks Oedipus to explain. Oedipus tells of Teiresias' words and Jokasta scoffs at them. No prophets are to be trusted. A prophet foretold that her child, her and Laios' child, would grow up to kill his father – but Laios was killed by strangers, at a crossroads where three roads meet. Instead of calming Oedipus, these words cause him more panic. He tells Jokasta how he once killed an old man at a crossroads, shortly before he came to Thebes. They decide to send for the only surviving witness to this murder (now an aged shepherd); his evidence will prove once and for all if Teiresias' words are true.

A visitor arrives from Corinth, to tell Oedipus that king
Polybos, the man he thought was his father, has died.
Triumphantly, Oedipus cries to Jokasta that this disproves
oracles – the god told him he would kill his father, and
Polybos has died of natural causes. But the Corinthian
reveals that Oedipus was not Polybos' son at all, but a
foundling; Jokasta suddenly realises the truth, and hurries
inside. After a brief interlude, the aged shepherd is
brought in and questioned. He speaks reluctantly: he was
the man who found the baby Oedipus and gave him
away, thinking that he must be a son of the royal house
of Thebes, possibly Laios' and Jokasta's own child.
Oedipus realises the truth: he is Laios' and Jokasta's son,
and he has murdered his father and mated with his
mother, exactly as the oracle foretold. He rushes into the
palace.

The Chorus sing of Fate, and how it can bring down even
someone as powerful and successful as Oedipus. A servant
hurries in: Jokasta has hanged herself, and Oedipus has
blinded himself with the gold pins from her dress. The
gates are thrown open, to reveal Oedipus, blind. He and
the Chorus lament what has happened. Kreon brings in
Oedipus' and Jokasta's daughters (Antigone and Ismene)
and Oedipus begs him to fulfil the curse Oedipus himself
laid on the murderer of Laios, and banish him from the
city. He says farewell to the children, and Kreon promises
to take care of them. The Chorus ends the play by
drawing a bleak moral: *Look at Oedipus and learn. Human
happiness means nothing. Count none of us happy until we're dead.*

Oedipus at Kolonos: **What Happens in the Play**

The play takes place in front of a sacred grove at
Kolonos, near Athens, several years after the events of
King Oedipus. Oedipus, blind and a beggar, is led in by his
daughter Antigone and sits down to rest. An outraged
villager orders him to leave the sacred ground, but is
persuaded to fetch Theseus, the Athenian ruler. Oedipus
prays to the gods to grant him peace at last, as
prophesied, but is interrupted by the Chorus of villagers
who treat him roughly despite Antigone's pleas.

Ismene, Oedipus' other daughter, arrives with news that
his two sons (Eteokles and Polyneikes) are about to fight
for supreme power in Thebes. The gods have said that
only Oedipus' return will save the city. Oedipus curses his
sons with extreme bitterness, praying that they will both
die in battle. Then he reveals his identity to the Chorus
who, horrified, advise him to make a ritual atonement;
Ismene goes into the sacred grove to perform this. The
Chorus question Oedipus about his 'crimes'. He asserts his
moral innocence.

Theseus enters and addresses Oedipus with courtesy,
offering him state protection against the Thebans; he, too,
goes to sacrifice.

After a Chorus celebrating the loveliness of Kolonos
(which was Sophocles' own birthplace), Kreon of Thebes
arrives with an escort of guards. Failing to persuade
Oedipus to return with him, he turns to force and his
soldiers take Antigone and Ismene as hostages. Theseus,
alerted by the noise, enters, confronts Kreon and compels
him to go with him to release the women.

Oedipus is reunited with his daughters and weeps as he thanks Theseus. The mood is broken by the arrival of Polyneikes, who begs his father to join him in attacking Thebes and defeating Eteokles. Oedipus, however, vehemently curses both his sons and predicts that each will kill the other.

As Polyneikes leaves, the Chorus hear thunder, an omen of Oedipus' coming end. Oedipus tells Theseus that his life will end in the sacred grove and offers to reveal mysteries which will protect Athens forever. They go into the grove, and after a while a soldier comes to report that Oedipus has miraculously disappeared; only Theseus was allowed to know the 'manner of his passing'. Theseus, Antigone and Ismene lead a ceremony of mourning.

Sophocles and Aristotle

Aristotle, in his *Poetics* (written a century after the great period of Athenian tragedy) drew conclusions about the nature and style of the form which almost immediately became canonical, as if they were rules rather than one man's observations. In essence, he said that a tragedy (as opposed to a historical account of the same events) tended to take place in a single location, and to involve the downfall of a powerful and 'fine' individual whose character is none the less flawed – a fatal flaw which causes him or her to challenge fate (as overseen by the gods) and to suffer for it. Witnessing this 'imitation of suffering', Aristotle said, allowed tragedy to 'purge' its spectators' emotions by inducing in them a combination of pity for the characters (or, as we might say, identification with them) and terror at the events depicted. Aristotle further pointed out that in the sequence of events depicted in tragedy, there was often a moment of recognition, when the main character realised that he or she was caught in self-constructed toils; from that point on, the movement to catastrophe was swift, inevitable and salutary.

Much of this is interesting rather than helpful. For all their later importance (*Poetics* is one of the most seminal statements ever made on the nature of tragedy), Aristotle's views have little relevance to those Greek tragedies which actually survive. (They are, for example, hard to apply in detail to any play of Aeschylus, and ignore the main kind of tragedy exemplified by Euripides' surviving work and by Sophocles' *Ajax*, *Philoctetes* and *Electra* – plays which show the minds and characters of people driven to extreme action by terrible circumstances, not always self-induced.) But the Aristotelian template does fit Sophocles' *Antigone* and *King Oedipus*. Aristotle himself praised *King Oedipus* more than any other play, and at one level it does fit his theories so closely that you could tick them off on a list. But it also deals with many ideas and uses many styles and dramatic methods not mentioned by Aristotle (who was arguing a specific, and rigorous, philosophical position, not writing literary criticism). It can hardly be overstated that Sophocles came before Aristotle, not the other way about, and that none of the Athenian poets whose works survive had any inkling of the Aristotelian 'rules' which were later to become so influential on writers of tragedy.

Original Staging

Sophocles' plays were first performed in the theatre of
Dionysos, at the foot of the Acropolis in Athens. They
were part of a competitive festival in honour of Dionysos,
god of drama. On each day of the festival a single author
produced three or four plays, before an audience of some
14,000 people. All the actors were masked. Three actors
(all male) divided all the speaking parts between them: in
King Oedipus, the leading actor probably played Oedipus,
the second actor Kreon, the Corinthian and the Servant,
and the third actor the Priest, Teiresias, Jokasta and the
Shepherd. The children were played by non-speaking
'extras'. In *Oedipus at Kolonos*, performed at the very end of
the 5th century, matters are less clear-cut. It is possible
that four actors were used; if there were only three, then
two of the characters (Theseus and Ismene) would have
been played by different actors at different points in the
play. In the one scene where four characters are on stage
together, one of them (Ismene) remains silent throughout
and could have been played by an 'extra'.

The Chorus, all male, consisted of 15 performers (a
number increased later to 25). They were drawn from all
districts of the city. To perform in a Chorus was a highly
regarded civic honour. The Chorus-men danced and sang,
and their leader occasionally took part in the spoken
scenes. There may have been musicians, playing *aulos* (a
reed instrument with a sound like an oboe), drum and
tambourine or finger-cymbals. As well as in the choruses,
music played a prominent part in the 'spoken' scenes, the
actors declaiming or singing at moments of high tension
or lyricism (marked in the surviving text by a movement

from iambic rhythms to more complex and varied structures). Something like one-sixth of *King Oedipus* was performed in this way, and the closing section of the play, in particular, makes dramatic use of the balance between spoken dialogue and song. In *Oedipus at Kolonos* too, there are scenes of heightened emotion (in particular, the final scene with the two sisters) in which music is essential.

All music and choreography were by Sophocles himself. The choreography closely followed the rhythm of the words which underlay the music; interaction between all three would have affected the way a playwright composed each scene. Sophocles supervised the production of his plays and may have had a hand in designing costumes and scenery. (Aristotle later said that Sophocles 'introduced' painted scenery to drama – a remarkable claim, particularly in view of the apparently sparse scenic demands of Sophocles' surviving plays, compared with those of his predecessor, Aeschylus.) Other playwrights took main acting roles in their productions, but by the time of *King Oedipus* Sophocles had retired from this aspect of his work.

At the festival performances, some playwrights (for example, Aeschylus) produced linked groups of plays: two, three or four on aspects of a single theme. (The *Oresteia* is a surviving example.) Others, including Sophocles, preferred plays with unrelated subject-matter. The final play in each group was a satyr-play, more musical than the others and featuring a Chorus of Satyrs, Dionysos' goat-footed followers notable for acrobatic dancing and sexual ribaldry. Sophocles – perhaps unexpectedly in view of his dignified modern reputation – was expert at this kind of play and his *Trackers* is one of the few surviving examples of the genre.

The Theban Myth Cycle

King Oedipus and *Oedipus at Kolonos* draw their plots from the foundation-myths of the city of Thebes. In myth, the city was miraculously founded by Kadmos, who killed a dragon, sowed its teeth and battled the warriors who grew from them. Generations later his descendant Laios offended the gods, and was told that his own son would murder him. This murder duly occurred and the son, Oedipus, compounded the family curse by taking Laios' throne and marrying his queen, Jokasta, Oedipus' own mother. *King Oedipus* focuses on the story of how Oedipus discovers the truth, and the terrible outcome of that discovery.

What happened next in the myth-story is in some dispute. The cycle appears to continue with the destruction of Thebes itself, by an army drawn from all the other cities of Greece, whose rulers were aghast at what had happened in the Theban royal house. But in Athenian drama, from the second half of the 5th century, a new twist was added – perhaps invented or elaborated by Sophocles himself. In this, Kreon, Jokasta's brother, acted as regent of Thebes until Oedipus' four children grew up. Then Eteokles and Polyneikes, Oedipus' sons, quarrelled about who should be king. Polyneikes gathered an army from Thebes' enemies, the people of Argos, and besieged the city. Eteokles led an army of Theban champions. The brothers fought in single combat, and each killed the other. Kreon ordered that Eteokles, defender of Thebes, should be buried nobly and that Polyneikes, the city's enemy, should be left to rot. When Oedipus' daughter Antigone disobeyed him, burying both brothers with equal honour, he punished her by burying her alive. This crime so outraged the rest of Greece that a second army was raised and the city was destroyed. Some scholars think that Sophocles, as well as developing the Antigone story, devised the plot of *Oedipus at Kolonos*, which rounds off Oedipus' life by bringing him old, blind and helpless to Athens, where he finally comes to terms with his destiny and disappears miraculously from mortal sight in Kolonos.

The Theban myths were not those preferred by Sophocles (over a third of his output was concerned with that favourite subject of all Athenian tragedians, the Trojan War and its aftermath) although they do account for almost half of the plays which happen to have survived. But the three 'Theban plays' were written independently: *Antigone* pre-dated *King Oedipus* by some dozen years and *Oedipus at Kolonos* followed nearly a quarter of a century later still.

King Oedipus

King Oedipus has a unique double status in Western literature and thought. On the one hand, thanks to Aristotle and Freud, it has a fame, a public recognition, second only to works such as *Romeo and Juliet* or *Faust*. Aristotle's detailed enthusiasm guaranteed it a reputation as one of the most 'achieved' and 'perfect' of all ancient tragedies, and Freud's attachment of its hero's name to one of his most controversial and seminal theories ensured that, for 20th century readers and theatregoers at least, it has an aura of psychological intensity and density which transcends anything actually said or done in the play itself.

On the other hand, it has been condemned as bloodless, schematic and implausible, and its singleminded intensity has been compared, to its detriment, with the wider concerns and more varied dramatic strategies of (say) Aeschylus' *Oresteia* and *Prometheus Bound*, Euripides' *Medea* and *Hippolytos* and Sophocles' own *Philoctetes* and *Electra*.

Reading or seeing the play nowadays, it can be difficult to experience it stripped of other people's agendas. Every word Aristotle writes about it can be justified from the text – and yet one feels, constantly, that he is narrowing his focus so much that he may be missing half the point. Rather than comment on the impact of the music, especially the choruses and the final scene, or on dramatic meaning, he prefers to go into niceties of rhythm. Similarly, he omits discussion of the religious and human side of things (which may well have bulked large in Sophocles' mind, to judge both by his surviving work and by what is known of his biography). He prefers an intellectualised ethical and philosophical analysis, which some people have dumped on the play itself. Above all, he seems unaware of the place in Sophocles' work of that quintessentially Athenian, not to say Sophoclean, component of all drama: irony. The result of all this is that an experience which is essentially fluid, suggestive, prismatic and open-ended is turned – not maliciously, but to serve purposes not primarily to do with drama as a performing art – into something hard-edged, polemical, selective and almost neurotically close-focused.

Aristotle apart, *King Oedipus* was by no means the most favoured of surviving tragedies, either in ancient times or right through to the 20th century. In Greece, plays about the Trojan War and its aftermath outstripped its popularity; in Rome and in those Renaissance European cultures which leaned on Rome, plays about Medea, Thyestes and other such gory subjects were far more popular. (There is, for example, no Shakespearean character which draws on Oedipus, as Lady Macbeth draws on Medea or *Richard III* and *Titus Andronicus* draw on Thyestes.) In 19th century Europe the most highly regarded of all Greek tragedies was not *King Oedipus* but *Prometheus Bound*. Even in the 20th century, despite the influence of Freud, *King Oedipus* became less a drama to experience than a vessel to freight with every kind of contemporary meaning, from existentialist angst to attacks on the nature and style of fascism.

In the theatre, all such matters, and criticisms of formalism or obsessive narrowness, tend to be swept away by the sheer power of the experience. The role of Oedipus is one of the finest in Western theatre, a marker for male leading men of all types and kinds – in English-speaking theatre, everyone from Herbert Beerbohn Tree to Laurence Olivier, from Charlton Heston to John Gielgud, from Orson Welles to Keith Michell, has made his mark on it. The coincidences and implausibilities which scholars find in the plot – why, for example, have Oedipus and Jokasta, who have been married for about a decade, only now begun to talk about, and see, the truth about each other, and themselves? – seem insignificant in the face of the inexorable momentum and 'irising in' of the dramatic narrative. The ironies, apparently so lumbering on the page, in the theatre can have electrifying effect. The choral odes, powerful enough in themselves, have crucial

importance for the articulation and emotional pacing of
the action. Above all, perhaps, the text seems to offer
entry points to a myriad of moral, religious, philosophical
and psychological ideas – overtones which may not always
be those imagined by later commentators, but which make
Sophocles' characters seem like voyagers travelling towards
their destiny in a ship manned by ghosts of every kind.
If the propositions stand that myth is not fixed but
protean and that its importance lies less in what it is than
in what people make of it, then few better demonstrations
could be found than the artistic, symbolic and intellectual
openness of Sophocles' treatment of these particular myths
in this particular play.

Oedipus at Kolonos

Oedipus at Kolonos was first performed in 401, five years after
Sophocles' death, and was probably a work of his extreme
old age. Many people find in it qualities of mysticism and
otherworldliness, claiming it to be the culmination of a
lifetime; they identify the playwright with his character
(just as Shakespeare, on the verge of retirement, is often
seen as the model for Prospero in *The Tempest*). Others
have compared the play to *King Lear* and see a kind of
progression from despair and horror to the acceptance of
necessity, an almost religious conversion. But these ideas
are not supported by the play's language or events.
Oedipus is not a very old man, merely soul-sick and
physically feeble; he is of a similar age to the two robust
city leaders, Theseus and Kreon, and the three of them
discuss and argue as equals. Oedipus' tenderness towards

Antigone and Ismene and his rage at Polyneikes and the absent Eteokles reflect the attitudes of the ancient world and are quite unlike the relationships of Lear to his daughters, which derive from his personality (and are psychologically more 'modern'). Oedipus' departure from the world and transfiguration are described in mystical terms, but they belong to the world of Olympian religious belief and Athenian folklore; we are invited to feel respect and awe but not sympathy for his character or his predicament.

Neither does the play deal with Oedipus' spiritual development; he goes into the grove the same man who arrived there, having stubbornly asserted his innocence, and his unrelenting hatred for his sons, from the start. He puts aside his anger and bitterness to face the reality of his own imminent death and the necessity of helping Athens, the city which has helped him. Sophocles is concerned not just with religion, man's relationship to the gods, but with political matters, too. Theseus, the ideal political leader (possessing personal qualities desperately lacking in Athens at the end of the fifth century), is balanced by the brutal and immoral Kreon, concerned only with political advantage for his city and himself.

The key event of the play is Oedipus' departure from life, but the focus of interest for Sophocles is *how* to die – the waiting, the preparation, the need to settle old scores, face new challenges and at the last to propitiate the gods. The other characters, however vivid, are seen entirely in relation to Oedipus – Antigone's anxious love, Theseus' compassionate protection, Kreon's bluster and arrogance, Polyneikes' pretended devotion. They remain substantially unchanged, but Oedipus constantly reveals new aspects of himself in the way he responds – contemptuous with Kreon, furious with Polyneikes, affectionate to his daughters. These transitions may be abrupt and untidy (not the kind of character-drawing which Aristotle approves), but they provide the mainspring of the action. In fact, *Oedipus at Kolonos* is unlike most other surviving Greek tragedies in that its subject is not so much the events of myth as the revelation of s single character at a moment of emotional and psychological crisis. Euripides' Medea and Sophocles' own Electra come close to this, but Oedipus in this play is perhaps the richest and most diverse antecedent of the complex characters of more recent drama.

Greek Exclamations

These are normally translated by such expressions as 'Woe is me!' or 'Alack'. They are in fact sounds rather than words, and were probably not meant to be exactly spoken. They may have been signs to the actors that some kind of wordless cry, almost musical, was intended: a brief melisma or vocal cadenza. *Yoh*, *aee*, *oee* and *moee* are all sounds of pain or grief. *Feoo* is a dismissive or deprecatory sound, roughly equivalent in use to modern Greek *po-po-po* or English clicking of the tongue. (In workshops we've found that an exhalation of breath can offer English-speaking actors a similar range of expression.) It indicates that the speaker is embarrassed by what is about to be said, or wants to change the subject from what has been said before. In a few places, I have expanded the 'vocal cadenza' idea by adding a line of the original Greek; pronunciation is indicated.

Kenneth McLeish

For Further Reading

The clearest (and clearest-headed) of a multitude of
scholarly books on Sophocles is H.D.F. Kitto, *Sophocles,
Dramatist and Philosopher* (1958) – Kitto is particularly good
at imagining Sophocles as a writer for the stage, embodying
his ideas not in tracts or treatises but in dramatic action.
The section on *King Oedipus* in Kitto's *Poesis* (1966),
similarly, is outstanding, among the least fussy and most
illuminating of all discussions of this most elusive play.
On Greek drama in general, recommended books are
Peter Walcot, *Greek Drama in its Theatrical and Social Context*
(1976), somewhat drily written but full of meat, and
Oliver Taplin, *Greek Tragedy in Action* (1978). Mary Renault,
The Mask of Apollo (1966) is a historical novel whose hero
is an ancient Greek actor; the book marvellously evokes
what it may have been like to play Greek drama in
ancient Greek theatres.

Sophocles: Key Dates

NB All dates are BC; many are approximate; dates of some plays are unknown.

c496 Sophocles born

490 Greeks defeat Persians at Marathon

480 Greeks defeat Persians at Salamis; Sophocles plays lyre at victory-celebration

468 Sophocles' first victory in dramatic competition (defeating Aeschylus)

450s *Ajax*

443 Sophocles appointed Treasury overseer during revision of tribute lists

c442 *Antigone*

440 Sophocles appointed General (with Pericles) to put down revolt on Samos

432 Building work completed on Parthenon and surroundings (including Theatre of Dionysos)

431 Outbreak of Peloponnesian War

c430 *King Oedipus*

428 Sophocles appointed General in war against Anaeans

c418 *Electra*

415 Athenians mount disastrous expedition against Sicily

412 Sophocles appointed to oversee restoration of political confidence after Sicilian debacle

c409 *Philoctetes*

406 Sophocles dies, aged about 90

404 Athenians surrender, end of Peloponnesian War

401 Posthumous first production of *Oedipus at Kolonos*

KING OEDIPUS

Characters

OEDIPUS, *ruler of Thebes*
PRIEST
KREON, *brother of Jokasta*
TEIRESIAS, *a blind prophet*
JOKASTA, *wife of Oedipus*
CORINTHIAN
SHEPHERD
SERVANT

Silent parts

CITIZENS
GUARDS
SERVANTS
ANTIGONE, ISMENE (*young children*)

CHORUS *of Thebans*

Notes. The Citizens at the start of the play are a small group, not the same people as the Chorus. 'Kreon' is not a name but a title ('His Honour'). A Glossary and Pronunciation Guide is given on pages 125–128.

Thebes. Open space outside the palace. A group of
CITIZENS *is waiting. Enter* OEDIPUS.

OEDIPUS. Thebans. My people. Children.
  What is it? Garlands, branches,
  Cries, prayers, incense on every altar –
  What d'you want of me? I'm here,
  In person: here, children, here,
  Your father, your saviour, your Oedipus.
  You, sir. Speak for them. What is it?
  Why are they here? Are they afraid?
  In need? I'll help them, do what I can.
  To ignore such a gathering, I'd be made of stone.

PRIEST. Majesty. Oedipus. Ruler of Thebes.
  We're at your feet. Old, young, fledglings.
  Priests – I of Zeus. Young men: warriors.
  Others kneel in the marketplace,
  In Athene's temple, in the fire-shrine.
  We're drowning, Majesty. Storm, blood, death.
  We're choking. Crops, parched.
  Animals, dead in the fields. Women, barren.
  Plague howls through the city, scours us.
  The Underworld grows fat on us.
  We're here, lord, not praying, you're not a god,
  Begging: your children, our father, you'll help us,
  We trust you, the storm of fate,

We trust you. You helped us before:
When the Sphinx was here,
Gulping our blood, you came,
You rescued us. A man, a mortal,
No different from the rest of us,
You knew what to do;
With God's help, you saved us.

Majesty, we're on our knees.
Help us, find a way now.
Ask the gods, ask mortals, act.
Your city, lord, save it, save it.
You helped us before, made us glad before,
Don't leave us now. 'He saved them once,
Then stood and watched them die' –
Don't let that be your story.
Don't rule a desert.
Your kingdom, Majesty, your people:
Steer us full sail, full cargo, not a ship of ghosts.

OEDIPUS. Dear children, little ones,
I knew you'd come. You're sick, in pain –
And none of you feels pain like mine,
Your king. You weep individual tears,
Each for yourself; I weep for all –
For you, for Thebes, for me.
I wasn't asleep; this isn't new to us.
For weeks we've wept,
Cudgelled our brains, thought what to do.
There was one way, one only. We did it.
His Honour, her Majesty's own brother –
We sent him to Delphi, Apollo's oracle,
To ask what I must do or say to save us.

He should be here. I'm surprised.
He's been away for days. I swear to you,
Whatever the advice he brings, God's word,
I'll do it. I'll obey it. I'll never flinch.

PRIEST. Your words give us hope.
And look: he's here. His Honour: here.

OEDIPUS. Apollo! He's smiling.
God grant good news.

PRIEST. A laurel-crown, full berried.
That means –

OEDIPUS. We'll ask him.

(*As* KREON *enters.*)

Your Honour. Brother-in-law. Good news?

KREON. None better. If we obey,
If we do as Apollo says, we're saved.

OEDIPUS. If, lord? There's doubt?
What *does* he say?

KREON. Shall I tell your Majesty inside,
In private, or here, where everyone –

OEDIPUS. Let everyone hear.
Their pain's my pain. Their burden's mine.

KREON. God's words, then, Majesty.
Apollo's words. There's cancer in the city.
Malignant. Diagnosed.
We must root it out, or die.

OEDIPUS. How root it out? What cancer?

KREON. Death, Majesty. A man's death.
   We must find the killer, and banish him
   Or give death for death.

OEDIPUS. Whose death?

KREON. Laios, Majesty. Before you came,
   Our lord before you came.

OEDIPUS. We know the name. Never knew the man.

KREON. We must find his killers and punish them.
   God's words.

OEDIPUS. Where, find? It's years ago.

KREON. Here, Majesty.
   'Look carefully, you'll find': Apollo's words.

OEDIPUS. This Laios – where was he killed?
   In Thebes? In the fields? Away?

KREON. He visited the oracle, they say,
   And never came back.

OEDIPUS. No witnesses? Fellow-travellers?

KREON. One, Majesty. The rest are dead.
   A poor witness, terrified.
   Only one small clue.

OEDIPUS. What clue?

KREON. A band of men, he said.
   Outlaws. Many hands. That's all.

OEDIPUS. Outlaws. The King?
   They wouldn't dare. Unless –

Hired killers? Was this a plot?

KREON. We didn't pursue it.
Laios was dead. We'd problems.

OEDIPUS. Your king was murdered
And you did nothing. What problems?

KREON. The Sphinx, Majesty.
More urgent than Laios.
The riddle of the Sphinx.

OEDIPUS. I'll settle this. I'll find the truth.
God's orders, Apollo's words, I'll do it.
For Thebes, for Apollo, I'll hunt this down.
I must. This touches us ourselves.
The old king dead – we could be next.
By helping Laios, we help ourselves.

Up, children.
Your garlands, your branches.
You: fetch the people. I'll do it.
With God's help, win or lose, I'll do it.

Exit.

PRIEST. We have what we asked.
He's promised. Apollo, fulfil your words.
Come down to us. Save us. Heal us.

Music. Enter CHORUS.

CHORUS. Sweet voice of God,
From Apollo's golden shrine,
What word for Thebes?
I shake, I cry.

Ee-AY-ee-e, DAH-lee-e, pe-AHN!
What's happening?
New pain? Old agony reborn?
Speak, child of golden Hope,
Immortal, speak!

Come down to us,
Athene, child of Zeus;
Bright Artemis,
Come down to us.
Apollo, archer, yoh! Come down,
Help us, save us now.
In the whirlwind of fate, of death,
You rescued us before –
Come, save us now.

Disaster, pain.
What's left for us?
No life, no green,
Dead children.
Our loved ones slip from us,
Shadows, smoke,
Ghosts in the dark of death.

Countless they lie,
Our city lies.
Dead corpses, weep for them
Wives, mothers.
Cry to the gods, cry, cry,
Help us, help,
Sweet gods, come help us now.

No clash of swords,
No hiss of spears –

Death, silent, stealthy,
He's here, he's here!
What darkness spares
Bright daylight snatches.
Zeus, father, strike him,
End him, the lightning-flash.

Apollo, come.
Bow springing,
Arrows dancing, dancing.
Artemis,
Bacchos lord of Thebes,
Dance him down,
Bright torches bring
And dance him, dance him down.

Dance. Music ends. Enter OEDIPUS.

OEDIPUS. Your prayers are answered.
   If you hear my words, hear and obey,
   Your prayers are answered.
   I know nothing of this murder. It's news to me.
   I came to Thebes afterwards. How could I know?
   But now, concerning Laios son of Labdakos,
   I make this proclamation: if anyone knows
   How he met his death, who murdered him –
   That person must speak, tell all.
   No need for fear: no punishment,
   Safe conduct from the city.
   Was it a stranger, a foreigner?
   Tell me the name, you'll be rewarded.
   But if you say nothing –
   To protect yourself perhaps,

Or one of your friends – be warned.
No one in Thebes, in all my lands,
Will speak to you, or shelter you,
Give water, food, a place at God's altar –
On pain of death. Banishment.
You caused this plague.
God speaks; I speak God's words.
Hear and obey.

As for the murderer –
One man or a member of a gang –
I curse him. Misery, life no-life.
And if he's mine,
If all unknowing I harbour him at home,
May all I pray for him be done to me.

Your task: obey. For me, for God, for Thebes.
Our country, torn, abandoned, cries out for this.
That such a man should die – your king –
And you do nothing! God orders it: find them.
I give my word, your king. I hold his throne,
His power, his wife (the mother of my heirs,
His own being dead, himself being . . . gone) –
I'll fight for him as they would, as if he were
My own dead father. Laios, son of Labdakos,
Descendant of Kadmos, Agenor, Polydoros,
I'll find your murderer. I'll make him pay.

Solemn words. Heed them, or suffer.
Those who turn away: parched crops,
Dead children, barrenness –
All they suffer now, and more.
Those who help, good people of Thebes,

May Justice and all the gods be with you now.

CHORUS. Majesty, your curse . . . I'll say what I can.
I didn't kill him. I've no idea who did.
Apollo ordered this. Perhaps the oracle –

OEDIPUS. If it chooses.
Who can force a god to speak?

CHORUS. Unless –

OEDIPUS. Say it.

CHORUS. Teiresias, Majesty.
God's voice on earth.
Perhaps he knows.

OEDIPUS. His Honour suggested that.
I sent for the man. Urgent messengers.
Twice. He's still not here.

CHORUS. There's nothing else.
Rumours . . . guesses.

OEDIPUS. What rumours? Even they might help.

CHORUS. Some said he was killed by passers-by.

OEDIPUS. Said, yes. No witnesses.

CHORUS. They'll come forward.
They'll hear your curse, and speak.

OEDIPUS. But not the murderer. He'll not fear words.

CHORUS. If anything's known, Teiresias knows it.
He's here, Majesty. They're bringing him:
God's voice, the voice of truth.

Enter TEIRESIAS, *led by a* SERVANT.

OEDIPUS. Teiresias,
    You know every secret, on earth, in heaven.
    You're blind, but you see, you understand.
    Our city's tottering; only you can save it.
    Apollo's words – those, too, you'll know:
    We'll die unless we find who murdered Laios,
    And punish them. Speak, Eminence.
    What secrets have you heard,
    From birds or other messengers?
    Tell us. Save yourself, your city, me.
    Put an end to it, the pollution
    We suffer for Laios' death.
    You have us in your hands.
    No finer work for a mortal than helping others.
    Speak, Eminence.

TEIRESIAS. Feoo, feoo.
    What use is knowledge,
    When it makes bad worse?
    I should have remembered.
    I should have stayed away.

OEDIPUS. What's the matter?

TEIRESIAS. Send me home, before it's too late
    For you, for me. Don't make me speak.

OEDIPUS. You know, and refuse to tell? You must.
    Your own city, Eminence: your Thebes.

TEIRESIAS. You've spoken, Majesty.
    Words of ill-omen.
    I won't add to them.

OEDIPUS. We're on our knees, Eminence.

TEIRESIAS. Don't ask me to speak. I won't.

OEDIPUS. So Thebes must die. Your fault.

TEIRESIAS. My pain if I speak. Your pain. I won't.

OEDIPUS. Coward! Traitor!
    You'd infuriate a stone!
    What kind of man are you?

TEIRESIAS. What kind of man are you, my lord?
    Your fury.

OEDIPUS. You spurn your own city, and I'm not to feel
fury?

TEIRESIAS. It's coming; it'll happen;
    My speaking won't stop it.

OEDIPUS. So, tell me. What difference does it make?

TEIRESIAS. Rage all you like, I'm dumb.

OEDIPUS. You go too far with me. I'll say what I think.
    I think, your Eminence, *you* had a hand in this.
    You planned it, you set it up,
    You'd have killed him yourself,
    If you'd not been blind.

TEIRESIAS. Is that what you think?
    You made a decree just now. Obey it.
    Not another word, to me, to them.
    The plague-bringer, polluter of Thebes,
    Is you.

OEDIPUS. You'll suffer for this.

TEIRESIAS. I speak what I know.

OEDIPUS. Who told you? Birds?

TEIRESIAS. You forced me to speak.

OEDIPUS. Again. Say it again.

TEIRESIAS. You want it clearer still?

OEDIPUS. I want no doubt.

TEIRESIAS. You're hunting a murderer.
    You've found him. You.

OEDIPUS. You'll feel pain for this.

TEIRESIAS. More fury, Majesty? Shall I say still more?

OEDIPUS. Say what you like. You're raving.

TEIRESIAS. Intimacy, hideous intimacy with her you love.
    You're floundering, Majesty, you're drowning –

OEDIPUS. And you, your Eminence: you're dead.

TEIRESIAS. The power of truth.

OEDIPUS. You're blind.

TEIRESIAS. You'll remember that word, Majesty.
    You'll hear it again. Then you, too, will see.

OEDIPUS. Night's all you know. Darkness.
    You can't hurt me, hurt those with eyes.

TEIRESIAS. God hurts, Majesty. Not prophets.

OEDIPUS. His Honour. He planned this.
    This work is his.

TEIRESIAS. Your work, Majesty.
　　Your own unaided work.

OEDIPUS. Money! Power! Fame!
　　How hobbled you are
　　With other people's envy!
　　They gave it me, this power I hold,
　　Gave it me freely, unasked, my city –
　　And now his Honour plots to steal it.
　　I trusted him, and he bribes this conjurer
　　To spirit it away, whose skill is blind,
　　Whose purse alone has eyes. You, tell me:
　　Who says you see so clearly?
　　Where were you then,
　　When the riddling Sphinx entwined our Thebes?
　　Your birds, your heavenly voices,
　　Where were they then?
　　When they needed a prophet,
　　A professional, *I* solved it.
　　Oedipus. I answered the riddle.
　　I alone. Native wit.
　　No birds, no magic. Brains.
　　And now you try to topple me.
　　You want to make his Honour king –
　　And bask in him.
　　You'll end this pollution? The pair of you?
　　If I didn't think you senile,
　　I'd teach you sense.

CHORUS. Your Eminence, he spoke out of turn.
　　You too, Majesty, your temper.
　　We need coolness, not fury,
　　To do what God commands.

TEIRESIAS. King you may be. But still I'll answer.
    Point by point. I demand it –
    I serve Apollo, I'm not your slave,
    And I owe his Honour no favours.
    You taunt me with blindness. But what of you?
    Where are your eyes, Majesty?
    You did what should not be done,
    You live where you should not live,
    You're married where you should not be married.
    You're drowning, Majesty.
    Don't you understand? You cancer them all,
    Your flesh and blood, the dead, the living.
    Your father, your mother:
    Their curse will bring you darkness
    Where now there's light,
    Will send you hurtling from Thebes,
    Headlong from Thebes.
    Where will they end,
    What hills won't echo them,
    Your shrieks, howls,
    When you know at last
    What parentage brought you here,
    What harbour of pain after such fair sailing?
    Agonies crowding, crowding,
    Yourself and your children,
    All one, all one.
    Shout how you like, accuse his Honour, me –
    No human being on Earth will match your fall.

OEDIPUS. Be quiet! Crawl home! Get out!

TEIRESIAS. You sent for me.

OEDIPUS. I sent for a prophet, not a madman.

TEIRESIAS. They'd not call me mad, your parents.

OEDIPUS. Now what does that mean? My parents?

TEIRESIAS. Today you were born, and today you die.

OEDIPUS. Another riddle.

TEIRESIAS. You boast you're good at them.

OEDIPUS. I earned this throne by them.

TEIRESIAS. And now you'll earn this pain.

OEDIPUS. I saved this city. You call that pain?

TEIRESIAS. I've no more to say. Boy, take me home.

OEDIPUS. Yes, take him. He scalds our ears.
Take him; dump him; make us clean of him.

TEIRESIAS. I'm not afraid. I'm safe from you.
I'll say it again, what I came to say.
The murderer, the man you're hunting
With all these oaths and threats,
The killer of Laios, is here in Thebes.
He thinks he's a foreigner. He's not.
He's a Theban, a native, and doesn't know.
He's drowning. He sees, and he'll be blind.
He's rich, he'll be poor. A proud man, a beggar.
He'll tap his way with a blind man's stick
In a foreign country. His children with him.
His sons his brothers,
His daughters his sisters,
His wife his mother,

His father his victim.
You asked for riddles. Solve these –
And then, if you can, say my prophecies are lies.

Exit. Exit OEDIPUS. *Music.*

CHORUS. God's word in sacred cave
Denounces him, criminal,
Crime of crimes, blood-hands,
Unspeakable. Who? Who?
Run, escape,
Galloping, galloping.
God's son pelts after him
In thunder, with lightning;
The Furies, untiring, hunt him down.

White snow on mountain peak –
A beacon, God's orders:
Track him down. Where? Where?
Bull, wild-eyed,
Snorting, high hills, forests,
Earth's deeps, far underground,
Cowering from heaven's eye
That hunts him, unsleeping, hunts him down.

Words of fear, fear them,
The prophet spoke:
How can we trust him?
We must, we must.
Hearts pound. We're blind.
Unheard-of – a quarrel? When?
Our Oedipus came from Corinth,
Rules Thebes, our Thebes.
We honour him. What does it mean?

Zeus knows, Apollo:
They understand.
Teiresias is mortal –
How can he know?
Proof, wait for proof,
Then believe it. The Sphinx,
When the Sphinx was here,
I saw it, he answered,
He knew. I won't condemn him now.

Music ends. Enter KREON.

KREON. People of Thebes, they say his Majesty
Is accusing me. I'm here, I'll answer.
If he thinks, as things now are in Thebes,
I've undermined him with words, or deeds,
If he offers proof, I'd rather die than live.
To be branded traitor – by his Majesty, by you,
By my own dear citizens! I'd rather die.

CHORUS. Wait, your Honour. Wait and see.
He was hot with fury.

KREON. I bribed that prophet to lie to him?
Is that what he said? And did he say why?

CHORUS. Your Honour, he gave no reasons.

KREON. But he meant it? He was . . . in control?

CHORUS. Your Honour: his Majesty. Ours not to question.
He's coming. Now.

Enter OEDIPUS.

OEDIPUS. You! Impudence!

You plot to kill me, steal
My throne from under me – and *visit* me?
Zeus above! D'you think I'm a fool?
Afraid? Did you think I wouldn't notice?
You dig a pit for me,
Under my nose, and think I'll fall?
That's not how kings are toppled, fool.
You need brains, money, accomplices,
To catch a king.

KREON. That's enough. Majesty.
You've made your charges.
Listen, now.
My turn to speak, to answer.

OEDIPUS. Speak, answer. You're good at that.
But I'm not good at listening – to traitors.

KREON. I said, listen.

OEDIPUS. I said, traitor.

KREON. You think no one's right but you,
No one else deserves hearing. You're mad.

OEDIPUS. You think you can undermine your king
And escape with your life. You're mad.

KREON. If that was true, I'd agree with you.
But what is it you say I've done?

OEDIPUS. You advised me, did you or didn't you,
To send for that . . . astrologer?

KREON. I'd do the same again.

OEDIPUS. How long ago did Laios . . . ?

KREON. What?

OEDIPUS. Meet his end?

KREON. Years ago.

OEDIPUS. And was that bird-interpreter in business then?

KREON. Highly respected, just as now.

OEDIPUS. So. *That* was when he mentioned me.

KREON. I never heard him.

OEDIPUS. This murder: you did enquire?

KREON. Of course we enquired.

OEDIPUS. So why did our learned friend say nothing?

KREON. I don't know. I can't explain.

OEDIPUS. You can. You know exactly.

KREON. What d'you mean?

OEDIPUS. He plotted this with you: to make this charge.

KREON. Is that what he says? Now, Majesty, *you* answer.

OEDIPUS. Your Honour, certainly. I didn't kill the king.

KREON. You married my sister?

OEDIPUS. Of course I did.

KREON. You share royal power with her?

OEDIPUS. Whatever she asks, is hers.

KREON. And I share that power, third among equals?

OEDIPUS. And first among traitors.

KREON. You don't know what you're saying.
   I want to be king, you say? I want to exchange
   A quiet life, easy sleep at night, royal rank,
   For the panic and turbulence of being king?
   Now, thanks to you, I've all I need.
   His Honour, revered, respected, safe –
   They smile to see me, they shake my hand,
   If they want your favour, they come to me,
   I bestow your bounty. All that you say I'd give
   For a crown, for the hedged-in life of being a king?
   A traitor? Ambitious? I'd not be such a fool.

   It's easily proved.
   Apollo, Delphi: go there, ask him.
   Was the oracle I brought the one he gave me?
   And as for Teiresias, that 'astrologer' –
   If you find any plot between his Eminence and me,
   Kill me. Put me to death. I'll guide your hand.
   But not on blind suspicion, Majesty. To know
   Our friends is as vital as knowing our enemies.
   When we drive out friends, we shrink our lives,
   Our own dear lives. To know an enemy,
   One day's enough; to know a friend takes time.

CHORUS. Fair words, Majesty. Take time to ponder –

OEDIPUS. He's poised to strike, and you say take time?

KREON. You want me out of Thebes?

OEDIPUS. I want you dead.

KREON. For nothing?

OEDIPUS. For ambition.

KREON. You're mad.

OEDIPUS. For justice.

KREON. Except for me.

OEDIPUS. A traitor.

KREON. You've heard nothing.

OEDIPUS. I've heard enough.

KREON. Dictator.

OEDIPUS. Thebes is mine.

KREON. Yours alone? Not mine?

CHORUS. Lords. Someone's coming.
   Her Majesty, Jokasta.
   Let her help you. Settle this.

Enter JOKASTA.

JOKASTA. Fools!
   This argument, what is it?
   The city's dying.
   Aren't you ashamed?
   Brawling like children.
   Majesty, go in. Your Honour, home.
   Have done with it.

KREON. Sister.
   His Majesty, your husband,
   Is trying to make up his royal mind:
   Is he to banish me, or kill me?

OEDIPUS. Exactly.
His Honour, your brother –
The schemer, the traitor. Trapped.

KREON. If this is true, if any of it's true,
Kill me. As God's my witness, kill me.

JOKASTA. Hear what he says, my lord.
For your sake, mine, the city's sake.

Music.

CHORUS. In God's name, Majesty –

OEDIPUS. What?

CHORUS. Respect his oath.
He called God's name.

OEDIPUS. You know what you ask?

CHORUS. I know what I ask.

OEDIPUS. Ask again.

CHORUS. An innocent man, a friend,
He swore in God's name.
Spare him.

OEDIPUS. And condemn myself?
To death? To exile?

CHORUS. No, Majesty.
By the Sun who sees all, knows all,
I don't mean that.
Our city's dying, tormented –
And now our princes quarrel, pain on pain.

Music ends.

OEDIPUS. So, spare him. And if I die of it,
If I'm driven out of the land I love,
On your head be it. Because you ask,
I do it. Not for him. Oh, not for him.

KREON. So merciful, so gracious!
You'll regret this. When your fury cools,
You'll regret it. You scald yourself.

OEDIPUS. In God's name, get out!

KREON. As you wish. They know I'm innocent.

Exit. Music.

CHORUS. Lady, go in.
Take his Majesty. Go in.

JOKASTA. First tell me what's happened.

CHORUS. Suspicion . . . accusation . . . unjust.

JOKASTA. From both?

CHORUS. From both.

JOKASTA. What words?

CHORUS. Lady, they're said.
As things now are,
They're best forgotten.

OEDIPUS. So old you are, so wise –
And all you do is blunt me.

CHORUS. Majesty, again I say it:
Fools only, madmen,

Would try to drag you down.
We were sinking before; you saved us,
You set us on course, you brought us home.
Now a second storm: we need you, need you.

Music ends.

JOKASTA. Husband,
Tell me. What is it?
This fury – why?

OEDIPUS. Wife,
I'll tell you.
His Honour's accusation.

JOKASTA. What accusation, to cause such rage?

OEDIPUS. Laios' murder. His Honour accuses me.

JOKASTA. There's evidence?

OEDIPUS. He spoke with another's mouth. A prophet.

JOKASTA. A prophet!
Husband, listen to me.
No human being on Earth
Need fear what prophets say.
I'll prove it.
A prophet came to Laios –
Not God, a prophet only –
And told him that one day his son,
His son and mine, would kill him.
But Laios was killed,
The whole world knows,
By strangers, at a crossroads,
Where three roads meet.

His son was exposed to die, at three days old:
We pegged his ankles and left him to die
Where no one ever went.
The prophecy was wrong.
The son never killed the father,
The father was not killed
By his own son's hand.
Ignore what prophets say!
What God wants us to know,
In his own good time, he'll tell us.

OEDIPUS. Wife.
What you said. I'm frightened.

JOKASTA. Husband,
What is it?

OEDIPUS. Where three roads meet, you said.
Laios was killed at a crossroads,
Where three roads meet.

JOKASTA. They said so at the time.
They'll say so still.

OEDIPUS. Where?
This crossroads, where?

JOKASTA. In Phokis.
Where the road from Daulia joins
The road from Delphi –

OEDIPUS. When?
When was he killed?

JOKASTA. A day or two before you came to Thebes.

OEDIPUS. O Zeus!
  What will you do to me?

JOKASTA. Oedipus, what is it?

OEDIPUS. Laios. Tell me.
  What did he look like?

JOKASTA. Tall. Greying hair. Like you.

OEDIPUS. Oee moee.
  Myself. I cursed myself.

JOKASTA. What is it?
  Husband. I'm frightened.

OEDIPUS. Not blind, the prophet.
  He saw, he saw.
  One more thing. Answer.

JOKASTA. If I can, I will.

OEDIPUS. Was he alone?
  Or was there a bodyguard,
  A royal bodyguard?

JOKASTA. Five men. One officer. The royal carriage.

OEDIPUS. Aee aee.
  I knew it. Jokasta, who told you?
  Who brought back news?

JOKASTA. The man who escaped. The only one.

OEDIPUS. He's here? Still in palace service?

JOKASTA. When he found you here,
  On his master's throne,

He begged me on his knees
To send him away,
Up-country, mountain pastures,
As far as possible.
A good man, loyal – I did as he asked.

OEDIPUS. Can they find him?
Find him and bring him?

JOKASTA. Of course. But husband, why?

OEDIPUS. Jokasta,
I said . . . what I should not have said.
Too much. I have to see this man.

JOKASTA. They'll fetch him.
But what's the matter?
Husband. Majesty.
Who else should you tell but me?

OEDIPUS. As you say.
If what I fear is true,
Who else should I tell but you?
Listen, then.
My father was Polybos of Corinth,
My mother Merope.
I was high-born, well-regarded.
One day . . . a strange thing . . . nothing . . .
A drunk at dinner said I wasn't my father's son.
I was angry, but did nothing then.
Next day I asked them,
My father and mother. They dismissed it.
A drunken insult, no more. I believed them.
But it lay there, the accusation.

Nagged my mind. In the end,
Without a word to my parents,
I left for Delphi, consulted the oracle.
The god made no straight answer,
Told me instead a prophecy beyond belief . . .
I was to murder my father,
Mate with my mother
And sire a brood that would sicken all who saw it.

I never went home.
Between me and Corinth,
I put the stars.
To prevent the oracle, the foulness.
I wandered . . . anywhere.
I came to the place
Where that king of yours, you say,
Was killed. Listen, Jokasta.
I'll tell you exactly what happened.
There was a crossroads. Three roads.
Servants, an outrider, a carriage.
Exactly as you describe.
They ordered me out of the way,
The lord, the officer. The coachman jostled me.
I lost my temper, hit him –
And the lord in the carriage
Lashed out at me, whip in the face.
I dragged him out, killed him.
Left him lying, and dealt with the rest of them.
If that was Laios, if that old man was Laios,
There's no one on Earth more cursed than I.
They must turn me away, no words, no shelter,
The whole of Thebes. My own decree. I killed,

And I sleep in the bed of the man I killed.
God's curse is mine. I cancer all I touch.
Exile. How can I go home, to Corinth,
To kill my father Polybos and mate with Merope
My mother? God's curse. Fate treads me down.
Zeus, light of day, let me not live to see it.
Let me slip away, vanish, wiped from the earth,
And never see that day, that cancer.

CHORUS. Wait, Majesty.
　　Wait till you hear the witness.

OEDIPUS. The shepherd. My only hope.

JOKASTA. How, hope, my lord?

OEDIPUS. His story. If what he says
　　Is the same as yours, I'm safe.

JOKASTA. What was it I said?

OEDIPUS. A gang. Passers-by.
　　Not one man, many.
　　If he says 'men', I'm safe. If not . . .

JOKASTA. He'll not change what he said.
　　He can't. I heard him, all Thebes heard him.
　　In any case, Majesty, even if Lord Laios
　　Was killed by a single man,
　　The prophecy still was wrong.
　　'His own son will kill him',
　　Apollo said. Laios' son, my son –
　　The baby we left to die.
　　Prophets, Majesty!
　　Don't give them the time of day!

OEDIPUS. I hear you.
> But still, the shepherd,
> Send someone to fetch the shepherd.

JOKASTA. As your Majesty pleases.
> Now, husband, come inside.

Exeunt. Music.

CHORUS. God give us reverence,
> In word and deed.
> There are laws, enthroned,
> High in Olympos,
> God's laws, born of no mortal,
> Unaging, eternal.

> Pride breeds the tyrant.
> Bloated, distended,
> Climbing the high peaks,
> Then falling, falling.
> No cure. God send us honour,
> For Thebes, protect us.

> Those who march in pride,
> Who fear no justice,
> Laugh at gods –
> Greed rules them,
> Dishonour –
> God's arrows, how will they dodge them?
> And if they do, if they slip free of fate,
> What use are these prayers, these dances?

> If oracles lie
> Why should we fear them?
> Not Delphi,

Shrine of shrines,
Olympia –
Zeus, god of gods, do you hear us?
Your power, Apollo's ancient power, denied.
The age of the gods is over.

Music ends. Enter JOKASTA, *with offerings*.

JOKASTA. My lords, these garlands, these offerings:
We go to pray. His Majesty's mind
Is distracted, ragged with terror:
His judgement's gone, he ignores what's past,
Refuses to listen to common sense,
Hears only what feeds his fear.
Apollo, lord, come down,
Be near. Accept these offerings,
Give us peace, calm our fear,
Our helmsman's distracted,
Oh help us, lord.

Enter CORINTHIAN.

CORINTHIAN. Friends.
I'm a stranger here.
His Majesty's palace?
Please tell me.
Or better than that,
Lord Oedipus himself.

CHORUS. It's here. He's here, inside.
And this is her Majesty, the queen.

CORINTHIAN. Lady, all happiness,
Yours and his Majesty's, forever.

JOKASTA. We return your greeting.
  You bring us news?

CORINTHIAN. I bring his Majesty good news.

JOKASTA. Where from, sir?

CORINTHIAN. Corinth. Joy mixed with tears.

JOKASTA. Explain.

CORINTHIAN. Your husband, Lord Oedipus:
  They want to make him king.

JOKASTA. In Corinth? But Polybos –

CORINTHIAN. Dead, lady. He lies in his grave.

JOKASTA. Oedipus' father, dead?

CORINTHIAN. As I stand before you.

JOKASTA. Slave, fetch his Majesty. Now.
  Oracles, prophecies, where are you now?
  This king my lord shunned all these years,
  For fear of killing him – he's dead. By Fate,
  Not by his Majesty's hand at all, by Fate.

  Enter OEDIPUS.

OEDIPUS. I grant your request, Jokasta.
  As you ask, I'm here. What is it?

JOKASTA. Hear this man,
  And then see what you think of oracles.

OEDIPUS. Who is he?

JOKASTA. He's from Corinth. Your father,

Lord Polybos, his Majesty – is dead.

OEDIPUS. Sir, is this true?

CORINTHIAN. True, Majesty. Lord Polybos is dead.

OEDIPUS. Assassination? Sickness?

CORINTHIAN. It doesn't take much to end an old man's life.

OEDIPUS. Sickness, then.

CORINTHIAN. Old age, my lord.

OEDIPUS. Feoo, feoo.
Jokasta, so much for birds and omens.
I was to kill my father. They said so.
And now he's dead, buried,
And I was here all the time,
My sword undrawn – unless
My absence killed him, makes me a murderer.
All those oracles, they're dead,
He's bundled them up
And taken them to Hades. Worthless.

JOKASTA. I said exactly so.

OEDIPUS. Fear blocked my ears.

IOCASTA. There's nothing left to fear.

OEDIPUS. My mother . . . mating with my mother . . .

JOKASTA. You're still afraid of that?
Fate rules our lives, not prophecy.
Live each day as it comes.
You're afraid of mating with your mother –
As thousands of men have done before you,

But in their dreams. Put it out of your mind,
Be easy.

OEDIPUS. Yes, if she'd died,
The mother who bore me.
But so long as she lives,
Whatever you say, I'll be afraid.

JOKASTA. Your father's dead.

OEDIPUS. It's her I fear.

CORINTHIAN. Excuse me, Majesty. Who is it you fear?

OEDIPUS. Merope, sir, the queen.

CORINTHIAN. Why, lord?

OEDIPUS. A fearful oracle.

CORINTHIAN. Can you tell a stranger?

OEDIPUS. 'You'll kill your father
And mate with your mother' –
Apollo's words. Ever since
I heard them, I've kept from Corinth.
Years. I've kept from my parents;
I've prospered.

CORINTHIAN. That fear kept you away?

OEDIPUS. That and killing my father.

CORINTHIAN. Majesty,
If I ended these fears forever . . . ?

OEDIPUS. Undying gratitude.

CORINTHIAN. It was for that I came –
   And to bring you home, my lord.

OEDIPUS. I won't go back to them, my parents.

CORINTHIAN. You still don't understand.

OEDIPUS. In God's name, tell me.

CORINTHIAN. You're afraid of *them*?

OEDIPUS. Because of the oracle.

CORINTHIAN. Afraid of double guilt?

OEDIPUS. The stain of it.

CORINTHIAN. Be easy, then.
   Lord Polybos was no relation.

OEDIPUS. Not my father?

CORINTHIAN. No more than I am.

OEDIPUS. You? How?

CORINTHIAN. Neither of us.

OEDIPUS. I was his son.

CORINTHIAN. You were a gift to him. From me.

OEDIPUS. He loved me.

CORINTHIAN. Before you came, he was childless.

OEDIPUS. A 'gift'. You . . . gave me.
   Did you buy me, or find me?

CORINTHIAN. I found you.
   In the woods. On Mount Kithairon.

OEDIPUS. You were travelling there?

CORINTHIAN. Tending sheep, my lord.

OEDIPUS. A shepherd.

CORINTHIAN. – who rescued you.

OEDIPUS. From what?
    What was wrong with me?

CORINTHIAN. Your ankles, Majesty –

OEDIPUS. They've been weak from birth.

CORINTHIAN. They were pinned together. I freed them.

OEDIPUS. I still have the scars.

CORINTHIAN. You were named for them, Majesty.
    Oedipus: Swell-foot.

OEDIPUS. Who pinned them?
    My father, my mother?

CORINTHIAN. The other man, perhaps.

OEDIPUS. What other man?

CORINTHIAN. The one who found you, gave you to me.

OEDIPUS. Who was it?

CORINTHIAN. He came from Thebes, he said.
    One of Laios' men.

OEDIPUS. Laios!

CORINTHIAN. This man managed the royal flocks.

OEDIPUS. Can I speak to him? Is he still alive?

CORINTHIAN. Your people know that, not I.

OEDIPUS. You, sir. You . . . you.
  Do any of you know
  The man he means, the shepherd?
  Is he here, still working?
  This whole thing hangs on him.

CHORUS. Majesty, you sent for him just now.
  It's the same man.
  Her Majesty will tell you.
  She knew him.

OEDIPUS. Jokasta?
  This *is* the same man?

JOKASTA. Don't ask.
  It's gossip. Not important.
  Leave it.

OEDIPUS. It could tell me who I am.

JOKASTA. In God's name, stop.
  For your own sake, stop now.
  You'll kill us both.

OEDIPUS. She may have been a slave, my mother –
  But why should that touch you?

JOKASTA. Majesty, on my knees, I beg you –

OEDIPUS. I'll know who I am.

JOKASTA. For your own sake, husband –

OEDIPUS. That's enough.

JOKASTA. Don't ask whose son you are.

OEDIPUS. Someone bring that shepherd.
    Let her go in and enjoy her snobbery.

JOKASTA. Eeoo, eeoo,
    THEES-teen-e.
    No more words.
    No more. No more.

    Exit.

CHORUS. She's gone, Oedipus.
    Her Majesty. Storms of grief.
    Silence. What's happening?

OEDIPUS. Storms, silence, I'll know who I am.
    She's highborn, ashamed of me, a slave.
    But I call myself Fate's child,
    The son of Fate
    Who gives all good to mortals.
    I'm not ashamed.
    My sisters are the seasons,
    My life in step with theirs.
    I am what I am,
    And I will know what I am.

    Music.

CHORUS. If I'm a prophet,
    See what's to come,
    Skilled in the ways of God,
    Tomorrow Kithairon will fill our song.
    Lord Oedipus is no one's son but yours:

You're his father, mother, nurse,
We'll dance for you, dance
Who gave us our our king.
Apollo ee-EH-i-e, hear us.

Who was your mother?
A mountain-nymph,
Immortal bride of Pan
Who walks the hills? Apollo loves our fields,
Our meadowland – was it he who fathered you?
Was it Hermes, who rules Kisthene,
Did Dionysos welcome you
From your mother's arms,
A nymph who dances on the hills?

Dance. Music ends. Enter SHEPHERD, *guarded.*

OEDIPUS. My lords,
I never saw the shepherd,
The man we sent for.
But this must be him. He's old;
My guards are bringing him.
You've seen him before.
Look, and say: is this the man?

CHORUS. Yes, Majesty.
One of Laios' most trusted slaves.

OEDIPUS. You: Corinthian.
Is this the same man?

CORINTHIAN. Yes, Majesty.

OEDIPUS. Old man, come here.
Answer directly.
Were you once Laios' slave?

SHEPHERD. Yes, Majesty.
Born in the palace.

OEDIPUS. What were your duties?

SHPHERD. I was a shepherd, Majesty.

OEDIPUS. On the plain, or far away?

SHEPHERD. Kithairon, sometimes.
Other places.

OEDIPUS. And this man here –

SHEPHERD. What man, Majesty?

OEDIPUS. D'you recognise him?

SHEPHERD. I . . . can't remember.

CORINTHIAN. It's hardly surprising, Majesty.
I'll remind him. Three summers
We spent together on Kithairon.
He had two flocks of sheep, I had one.
When winter came, we separated:
I drove my animals back to Corinth.
He brought his home, here,
To Laios' folds. Is this not true?

SHEPHERD. Years ago. I think so.

CORINTHIAN. And d'you remember the child,
The child you gave me,
To bring up as my own?

SHEPHERD. What child?
What d'you mean?

CORINTHIAN. He's grown up now.
  This man: his Majesty.

SHEPHERD. You're lying.
  Go to Hell. You're lying.

OEDIPUS. Control yourself.
  You're lying.

SHEPHERD. Master, my dear, I'm not.

OEDIPUS. You deny what he says about the child?

SHEPHERD. It's nonsense.

OEDIPUS. Tell the truth, willingly, or –

SHEPHERD. Majesty –

OEDIPUS. Take him.

SHEPHERD. Majesty, I'll tell you.

OEDIPUS. You gave him the child he speaks of?

SHEPHERD. Yes, Majesty.
  I should have hanged myself.

OEDIPUS. Tell the truth, or you'll still be hanged.

SHEPHERD. Majesty,
  If I tell what I know, I'm dead.

OEDIPUS. Take him away.

SHEPHERD. No, Majesty.
  I told you: I gave him the child.

OEDIPUS. Where did you get it?
  Was it your own? Someone else's?

SHEPHERD. Someone else's.

OEDIPUS. Whose?
  Tell me.

SHEPHERD. Majesty, don't ask me.

OEDIPUS. Tell me. Whose child was it?

SHEPHERD. They say it was a child . . . of Laios' house.

OEDIPUS. A slave's? Someone else's? Answer!

SHEPHERD. Majesty, I daren't.

OEDIPUS. You must.

SHEPHERD. If I speak, I'll die.

OEDIPUS. And I if I hear. But hear I must.

SHEPHERD. They said it was . . .
  His own son. His Majesty's son.
  She'll tell you, her Majesty, inside.
  She'll tell you.

OEDIPUS. She gave you the child?

SHEPHERD. Yes, Majesty.

OEDIPUS. With what orders?

SHEPHERD. Majesty, to kill.

OEDIPUS. His own mother?

SHEPHERD. There was an oracle.

OEDIPUS. Oracle?

SHEPHERD. That he would kill his parents.

OEDIPUS. You gave him to this old man?

SHEPHERD. I pitied him, Majesty.
　　I thought,
　　'I'll send him away, far away.'
　　This man took him, saved him –
　　Doomed him.
　　If you're who he says you are,
　　Majesty, you're doomed.

OEDIPUS. Eeoo, eeoo.
　　Now I see, I know.
　　Born where I should not have been born,
　　Killing where I should not have killed,
　　Mating where I should not have mated:
　　Now at last, I see.

　　Exeunt all but CHORUS. *Music.*

CHORUS. Who lays true claim to happiness?
　　In the grey dawn we wake, we know
　　How all our joy was smoke, was dream.
　　Look now at Oedipus, at mortal fate.

　　How proud he stood, how high! He broke
　　The subtle Sphinx, he was a tower,
　　A lighthouse, in the agony of Thebes:
　　He was Majesty, master, lord of lords.

　　He strode the peaks, he fell.
　　Disaster, pain,
　　His mother's husband,
　　His children's brother –
　　Hidden, hidden in the dark.

Time found him out. Time saw.
Time brought him down.
Weep for his honour lost,
Who dazzled us, destroyed us,
The Majesty of Thebes.

Music ends. Enter SERVANT.

SERVANT. Lords, great ones,
It's happened, such things, such foulness,
The palace, inside, it's happened.
Rivers, washing, foulness,
It's there, it's there. They're hiding,
They're coming, we'll see them,
We'll shut our eyes, we'll see them.
They did it.
They hurt themselves,
They did it, they did it.

CHORUS. We know what we know.
What could be worse than that?

SERVANT. I'll tell you. Tell you.
Her Majesty, Jokasta, her Majesty,
Is dead.

CHORUS. Poor lady. How?

SERVANT. Her own hand.
She did it. You haven't seen,
Don't know . . . I'll tell it,
Her agony, every detail.
She ran like a wild woman.
Hooks of hands, tearing at her hair.
Across the courtyard. Inside.

She barred the door.
She screamed at Laios,
His Majesty long dead,
His child, his son
Who was to kill the father
And mate with the mother,
Man-child, child-man, brother-father . . .
Silence.
Nothing else.
She died.
We didn't see.
His Majesty burst in, our eyes were on him,
Watching him, we didn't see her die.
He was shouting, running, room after room.
'A sword! Where is she?
Wife no-wife. Mother-mistress.
Seedbed.'
None of us moved.
Some god showed him the way.
He was howling, a hunting dog.
He smashed down the door,
Burst the bolt from the socket –
And there she was, dangling,
A pendulum.
He bellowed like a bull.
Unfastened her, laid her on the ground.
Then . . . There were pins,
Gold pins, fastening her dress.
He snatched them, stabbed his eyes,
Shouting 'See nothing now. Not see
What I did, what they do to me,
Not see, not see.

Darkness. See dead. Not living see.'
Each word, he stabbed and stabbed.
Blood spurted, poured,
White cheeks, black beard, red matted, red.
That's how it is with them:
His Majesty, her Majesty.
How blessed they were, how happy –
Now death, tears, pain, all's theirs.

CHORUS. Where is he now?

SERVANT. Inside. Shouting.
'Open the door. Show them.
The people, show them.
His father's murderer.
His mother's – I won't say it.
Banish me, drive me away,
My judgement, the curse I spoke.
I'll not stay here.'
His strength has gone.
He's blind. Crushed.
They're opening the doors.
See for yourself.
A sight to turn all loathing into tears.

Music. OEDIPUS *is revealed.*

CHORUS. All human pain is here.
Why, lord, why? Such madness,
Such pouncing on disaster.
Which god bears down on you?
Feoo, feoo.
I can't bear it. Can't bear to look.
So much to ask, to say to you –
And I shudder, I turn away.

OEDIPUS. Aee aee. Aee aee.
  Feoo feoo.
  THEEStanoss eYOH.
  Where now? Where go now?
  I hear my own voice, fading.
  God, where are you taking me?

CHORUS. To a place
  None may speak of, none may see.

OEDIPUS. Yoh.
  Darkness.
  It billows,
  It fills, it chokes.
  Oee moee.
  Stabbing, pins,
  Pain,
  What I did to them.

CHORUS. Pain on pain, your agony,
  The torment of those you loved.

OEDIPUS. Yoh.
  You're here,
  My friend, still my friend.
  Feoo feoo.
  Stayed by me.
  It's dark.
  I recognise your voice.

CHORUS. How could you bear it?
  Your eyes, your own eyes?
  What god was this?

OEDIPUS. Apollo's words, his oracle,
    My hands, no one else, these hands.
    Why should I see?
    Ugliness. I need no eyes.

CHORUS. It's as you say.

OEDIPUS. What have I left to see,
    To hear, to love?
    Take me away. Please,
    Take me, I'm dead,
    God's cursed me, dead.

CHORUS. What you did,
    What's happened here –
    Why did you live to solve this riddle?

OEDIPUS. Damn him, damn him who found me,
    Unpinned my ankles, saved me.
    I should have died then, not lived
    To savage those I love.

CHORUS. What you say is true.

OEDIPUS. No father-killer then,
    Mother-husband.
    God's enemy, their son,
    The cursed ones,
    Their brother, my children.
    Evil outrunning evil.
    All foulness, its name is Oedipus.

    Music ends.

CHORUS. Even so, Majesty –
    To blind yourself! Does any crime
    Deserve such punishment?

OEDIPUS. Enough!
    Enough wise counsel!
    What I did was right.
    Was I to use these eyes to look on him,
    There in the Underworld, the father I killed,
    Or on her, my mother? For what I did to them
    I should be ripped apart.
    My children, was I to smile at them,
    Sown where I sowed them? What eyes have I
    For Thebes, my Thebes, its towers, its temples?
    Its king! I tore myself from Thebes:
    I cursed myself, decreed my own exile,
    Unclean, unclean,
    Laios' son who fouled the gods.
    Eyes, ears –
    I should dam up my ears,
    Seal myself, silence, darkness.
    No more hurting.
    Why, Kithairon, yoh?
    Why shelter me, not kill me,
    Why let me come to Thebes?
    Corinth, Polybos I called my father,
    Why didn't you see, destroy,
    The festering soul, your princeling?
    Crossroads, three roads,
    A stand of trees, you drank his blood,
    My father's blood, my own heart's blood,
    I poured it,
    You drank and drank, remember?
    I came to Thebes, I married.
    Married! Seed, blood-seeding seed,
    The father, mother, wife,

The husband-son,
The children-brothers-sisters,
All one, all evil.
I did it, won't speak of it.
Foulness. In the name of God,
Hide me, kill me, drown me,
The sea, all gone, away.
Over here.
Touch me. It's all right.
You're frightened. Don't be.
My sin, *my* guilt, it's not contagious.

Enter KREON, *with* SERVANTS *bringing two small
children,* ANTIGONE *and* ISMENE.

CHORUS. His Honour's here.
    He'll hear your prayers, decide what to do.
    His Honour: as things now are,
    He holds all power in Thebes.

OEDIPUS. Oee moee.
    How can I ask him?
    After all I did, I said,
    What can I say to him?

KREON. Oedipus, I won't laugh at you,
    Throw back in your face
    What you said before.
    You men: respect your fellow-citizens,
    Respect the Sun above, lord of all life.
    Neither he, nor the cleansing rain,
    Nor Mother Earth, should see
    This foulness. Take it inside.

Let those it most concerns,
Its own relatives, ourselves, take care of it.

OEDIPUS. Wait. Such kindness,
So unexpected, so undeserved.
One favour. For your own sake, Majesty, not mine.

KREON. What is it you ask so humbly?

OEDIPUS. Banish me. Now.
Where no one in Thebes will see me.

KREON. We await Apollo's orders.

OEDIPUS. It was clear enough.
The oracle. The father-killer must die.

KREON. Things are different now.
We must ask again.

OEDIPUS. About . . . this?
The gods' plaything? Ask what?

KREON. They decide, and we obey.
You know that now.

OEDIPUS. I order you, then . . . I beg you . . .
Her Majesty, inside,
Bury her, funeral rites.
Your sister, Majesty.
As for me, send me away,
Send me far from Thebes.
Kithairon, there let me live, there die.
They chose it, my father, my mother.
They wanted me dead: I'll die.
How, I don't know.

No sickness will end my life, nothing ordinary.
Something strange, terrible – I've been saved for that.
Well, let it come.
Your Honour, one more thing: the children.
Not the boys, they're grown,
They can look after each other,
My daughters. My poor little girls.
They sat beside me,
Never ate a meal
Without their father, shared all I had –
Take care of them.
Let me hold them, stroke them.
Your Honour, Majesty,
They're here. It's as if I saw them.
They're crying. I hear them.
You did it. You pitied me,
You did it. My darlings.
Let me touch them, speak to them.

KREON. I know what they mean to you.

OEDIPUS. God reward you, a better fate than mine.
Darlings, where are you? Come here.
Let me hold you, your brother's hands.
They stole your father's eyes, his bright eyes,
Your father knew nothing, saw nothing,
Sowed you where he himself was sown.
I'm crying for you: look.
I can't see you. I see your future.
Bitterness, unhappiness.
On the city's feast-days, what will you do?
Shouting, dancing. You'll sit at home in tears.
When you're old enough to marry,

Who'll have you? Who'll take you
For what you are, forget your father
Who killed where he should not have killed,
Married where he should not have married,
Made children where he was made?
That's what they'll say.
You'll die unmarried, dry old maids.
Majesty, Menoikeus' son, we're dead,
Their parents. You're all they have.
Be kind to them. Don't make them
Outcasts, beggars, wanderers.
Don't make them me.
They're little girls. Your sister's children.
Be kind to them. Say yes, Majesty.
Touch my hand.
Antigone, Ismene, I won't say more.
When you're older, you'll understand.
Be happy. Be happier than me.

KREON. Enough now. Go in.

Music.

OEDIPUS. No choice.

KREON. It's time.

OEDIPUS. You know what I ask?

KREON. Ask again, as we go inside.

OEDIPUS. Send me far from Thebes.

KREON. God's choice, not mine.

OEDIPUS. Cursed by God, I go.

KREON. They'll give what you ask.

OEDIPUS. You know this?

KREON. I promise nothing.

OEDIPUS. Take me inside.

KREON. Leave the children.

OEDIPUS. No! No!

KREON. Give no more orders.
  You were powerful once; no more.

CHORUS. People of Thebes, see: Oedipus.
  He solved the riddle. He ruled this land.
  All envied him. His power, his wealth.
  Now the storms of life have swamped him.
  Look at him now, and learn:
  We're mortal. Count none of us happy
  Till we come, untroubled, to the day we die.

  Exeunt.

OEDIPUS AT KOLONOS

58

Characters

OEDIPUS, *formerly ruler of Thebes*
ANTIGONE, *his daughter*
VILLAGER *of Kolonos*
ISMENE, *daughter of Oedipus, sister of Antigone*
THESEUS, *ruler of Athens*
KREON, *acting ruler of Thebes, brother-in-law of Oedipus*
POLYNEIKES, *elder son of Oedipus*
SOLDIER

SOLDIERS *(silent parts)*

CHORUS *of villagers*

Note: A Glossary and Pronunciation Guide is given on pages 125–128.

A grove of trees in the village of Kolonos. Enter OEDIPUS *and* ANTIGONE.

OEDIPUS. Child. Antigone. Where are we?
  Where in the world is this?
  A blind old man, a tramp –
  Who'll help me today?
  Small charity, I don't need much.
  They give less than I ask; it's enough.
  I've learned: an old man, a king, in pain –
  I've learned.

  Child, can you see anywhere?
  Somewhere to sit down –
  Beside the road? A grove of the gods?
  Help me sit. We must find out where we are.
  Someone else's town: we must do as they say.

ANTIGONE. Father, unhappy Oedipus,
  In the distance there are walls, battlements.
  I can just make them out.
  These trees are some sacred place. It's obvious:
  Laurels, olives, vines; nightingales singing.
  Sit here on this rock. An old man:
  You've come a long way.

OEDIPUS. Help me. Show me. I can't see.

ANTIGONE. I know what to do. I've learned.

OEDIPUS. Can you see where we are?

ANTIGONE. Somewhere near Athens, that's all I know.

OEDIPUS. They said Athens, the people we met?

ANTIGONE. Shall I find someone, and ask?

OEDIPUS. Yes, child, if there's anywhere. Houses.

ANTIGONE. It's all right. Someone's coming.
No need for me to go.

OEDIPUS. Who's coming? Where is he?

Enter VILLAGER.

ANTIGONE. Here now. In front of you. Ask him.

OEDIPUS. Sir, my daughter sees for us both.
She says you may be able to tell us –

VILLAGER. Get up! You can't sit here.
You mustn't. No one's allowed here.

OEDIPUS. This is a sacred place?

VILLAGER. Forbidden. No entering.
No living. Their place:
Night's daughters, daughters of darkness.

OEDIPUS. Tell me their names. I'll honour them.

VILLAGER. The Kind Ones, we call them.
All-seeing Ones. They have other names.

OEDIPUS. May they welcome me.
This is the place. It was here;

It was fated, here.

VILLAGER. What was fated?

OEDIPUS. My resting-place.

VILLAGER. I can't throw you out.
Not without orders. I'll go and ask.

OEDIPUS. In God's name, don't hurt me, sir.
A poor old man, a wanderer. Just tell me –

VILLAGER. I'll answer. Ask.

OEDIPUS. What is this place?

VILLAGER. As much as I know, I'll tell you.
The whole area's sacred: to Poseidon, Sea-lord,
To Prometheus, Fire-bringer. But this place,
Here where you're standing –
They call it Bronze Floor, the Entrance.
It protects the city, our Athens.
Kolonos Horse-tamer's our guardian.
His statue's here. They call this place
Kolonos, after him. It's famous,
Not just in stories. The villagers –

OEDIPUS. People live here?

VILLAGER. In the village, yes.
Kolonos' people.

OEDIPUS. Who rules them?

VILLAGER. His Majesty in Athens.

OEDIPUS. Which Majesty?

VILLAGER. Theseus, son of Aigeus.
　His father was king before.

OEDIPUS. Can someone take him a message?

VILLAGER. What message?

OEDIPUS. That if he does me service,
　He'll win great profit.

VILLAGER. From you?
　From a beggar, a blind man?

OEDIPUS. He'll find my words have eyes.

VILLAGER. All right. You look honest enough.
　I'll go. Wait there, where I found you.
　I'll tell them, I'll go to the village:
　They'll decide if you can stay,
　Or if you have to go.

　Exit.

OEDIPUS. Antigone. He's gone?

ANTIGONE. Yes, father. Speak freely.
　There's no one else here, just me.

OEDIPUS. Fearful ones, dread eyes,
　Who see, who see,
　Your holy ground I touch,
　First in this land.
　Be kind to us, in Apollo's name –
　We come in Apollo's name.
　God spoke to me:
　'You'll wander, much suffering.
　You'll come to their holy place,

The Dread Ones, your resting place.
Your life on earth will end,
Your pain will end,
Good luck you'll bring to the people there,
Destruction and death
To those who exiled you.'

Wonders he spoke of,
Signs, to welcome me:
An earthquake, lightning,
Clear signs from Zeus.
This is the place, this holy place.
You brought me here, you guided me –
How else could I have come?
Goddesses, help me, accept me.
Apollo promised.
Bitter suffering, more than all endurance.
Help me.
Sweet daughters of ancient Dark,
Smile down on me,
Smile down on me Athens,
Most cherished of cities.
Not Oedipus entreats you:
His husk, his shadow, entreats your help.

ANTIGONE. Hush. They're coming.
Old men. Looking for you.

OEDIPUS. I'll hide among the trees,
I'll hear what they want.
Help me, child. We'll listen,
We'll see if it's safe.

They hide. Music. Enter CHORUS.

CHORUS (*separate voices*). This way. Who is it? Where?
  Impudence! He's hiding.
  Find him, look for him,
  Check everywhere.
  A stranger, an outsider –
  Who else would trample holy ground?
  Their ground: dread goddesses,
  Their names unspeakable –
  Look away, turn away, pray silent prayers.
  A stranger, a foreigner,
  Dirties them, dishonours them –
  Where is he? Where?

OEDIPUS (*from hiding*).
  I'm here. I'm blind:
  My ears are my eyes.

CHORUS. Eeoh eeoh,
  Don't look at him. Don't hear him.

OEDIPUS. I'm harmless. Help me.

CHORUS. Zeus keep him away. Who is he?

OEDIPUS. Unenviable. Most miserable.
  Guardians, I see with another's eyes.
  I'm a grown man, I lean on a child.
  Look.

  He reveals himself to them.

CHORUS. Ee-eh! Your eyes! You're blind!
  Were you born so? Old man,
  Long life, long misery,
  We see it, see it.

You don't understand – how could you? –
You're in danger. Come out of there.
Their trees, their silent trees,
Their stream, their honey,
Come out. You've pain enough to bear.
Don't you hear me? Come out.
You're exhausted. It's holy ground.
Come out, talk here.

OEDIPUS. Child, Antigone.
  What must we do?

ANTIGONE. Father, respect them.
  Do as they say.

OEDIPUS. Help me.

ANTIGONE. I'm here.

She leads him out.

OEDIPUS. Don't hurt me, sirs.
  I'm in your hands.

CHORUS. Old man, be easy.
  No one will force you.

OEDIPUS. Over here?

CHORUS. Further out.

OEDIPUS. This far?

CHORUS. Help him, child. See for him.

ANTIGONE. Father, this way.

CHORUS. Rash man. Don't you know?

Don't you understand?
Respect what we respect.

OEDIPUS. Child, show me.
I'll talk to them,
Hear what they say,
Respect them.

CHORUS. That rock. No further.

OEDIPUS. Over here?

CHORUS. You heard me.

OEDIPUS. May I sit?

CHORUS. On the edge. Be careful.

ANTIGONE. Father, my hand.
Put your foot there . . . there . . .

OEDIPUS. Eeoh moee moee.

ANTIGONE. Lean on me.

OEDIPUS. Oh moee, that I should come to this.

He sits.

CHORUS. Poor old man, be easy.
Who are you? This patient girl,
Who is she? Where do you come from?

OEDIPUS. Nowhere. You mustn't. Don't –

CHORUS. What's wrong?

OEDIPUS. Don't ask my name. I can't.

CHORUS. What's the matter?

OEDIPUS. I'm accursed.

CHORUS. Tell us.

OEDIPUS. Child, oh moee, help me.

CHORUS. Your father's name − ?

OEDIPUS. Oh moee, Antigone, help me.

ANTIGONE. Tell them, father.
    What else is left?

OEDIPUS. No more hiding.

CHORUS. Speak.

OEDIPUS. You see *his* son, Laios' son . . . Oh −

CHORUS. Eeoo eeoo.

OEDIPUS. Laios son of Labdakos.

CHORUS. Oh Zeu . . .

OEDIPUS. See Oedipus, accursed.

CHORUS. You − Oedipus?

OEDIPUS. Don't be afraid.

CHORUS. Eeoh oh oh.

OEDIPUS. Accursed.

CHORUS. Oh oh.

OEDIPUS. Child, what's happening?

CHORUS. Out. Get out.

OEDIPUS. You promised me.

CHORUS. God understands.
    You cheated us,
    You hid your name.
    Like for like: we'll cheat you. Out.
    You pollute this holy place.

ANTIGONE. My lords, I beg you.
    When you heard his name, my father,
    You refused to listen,
    To hear what he did,
    What he was forced to do.
    But me, lords,
    Oh pity me. I beg you,
    Tears in my eyes –
    They could be your daughters' eyes –
    Have mercy. We've nothing.
    You're all we have,
    You're gods to us, we need you.
    Help us. In the name of all you love,
    Homes, families, possessions, gods –
    Don't drive us away.
    We're human beings, we're mortals –
    God's ruined us, how could anyone avoid it?

    Music ends.

CHORUS. Daughter of Oedipus, we pity you.
    We pity your father, his suffering.
    But we're afraid. God's fury –
    We daren't say more.

OEDIPUS. Reputation!
    It's smoke on the breeze, it's gone.
    Athens, the most compassionate place

In all the world,
Most god-fearing –
Until a stranger comes,
Wretched, in need,
Only you could help,
And you send him packing.
I sat here, I sheltered here,
And you drive me out
As soon as you hear my name.

It's a shadow, it isn't real.
You're afraid of what I did –
My father, my mother,
Of what I did to them?
I didn't choose it.
What else could I do?
I killed in self-defence,
He struck the first blow.
I didn't know his name –
And even if I had,
I'd have been justified.
It wasn't planned,
It wasn't my choice.
They chose, who pinned their baby's legs
And left him to die. They chose.

In God's name, help. You promised.
'Come out', you said. 'You're safe.'
Do as your gods do. If we're honest,
They respect us, if we're not, they hunt us,
We don't slip free. Do as they do.
Don't darken Athens' name. I trusted you.
Your mercy: I'm in your hands, help me.

Don't flinch from these eyes.
A god-fearing man, I bring you good.
When Theseus comes, when your king arrives,
I'll tell him. You'll hear, you'll know. Till then,
Don't break your word: be kind to me.

CHORUS. We're afraid.
We don't know what to do.
We'll wait for his Majesty.
He'll know.

OEDIPUS. Where is he?

CHORUS. Someone's gone to fetch him:
The man who found you here.

OEDIPUS. And he'll come, his Majesty?
For a beggar? Put affairs of state aside, and come?

CHORUS. When he hears who you are, he'll come.

OEDIPUS. That messenger didn't know me.

CHORUS. News flies – all the way to Athens.
Passers-by: they'll have heard, they'll tell.
The whole world knows you. He'll come.
Even if he's asleep, he'll hear, he'll come.

OEDIPUS. God make it worth his while:
For him, for Athens, God bless them both.

ANTIGONE. Oh Zeus. Father.

OEDIPUS. Child, what is it?

ANTIGONE. There, on the road.
A woman, riding. Travelling-clothes,

A sun-hat – it must be – it is –
She's smiling, waving – it has to be –
Ismene!

OEDIPUS. What?

ANTIGONE. My sister, your daughter. Ismene.
You'll hear her voice. You'll know.

Enter ISMENE.

ISMENE. O father. Antigone.
At last, I've found you at last.
Look: I can hardly see you.
Tears of happiness.

OEDIPUS. Ismene, darling.

ISMENE. Father, O father.

OEDIPUS. You found us.

ISMENE. I searched and searched.

OEDIPUS. Touch me, child.

ISMENE. Let me hug you both.

OEDIPUS. Daughters. Sisters.

ISMENE. Who can live like this?

OEDIPUS. Like her? Like me?

ISMENE. All three of us.

OEDIPUS. Why did you come?

ISMENE. Father, for you.

OEDIPUS. To see me?

ISMENE. And to tell you news.
I took one loyal slave, and came.

OEDIPUS. Your brothers: they stayed at home?

ISMENE. They stayed.

OEDIPUS. In Egypt, they say, men send
Their women out into the fields to work,
While they sit inside and spin. So it is with us.
My daughters support their father,
Shoulder his burdens; my sons sit at home
Like little girls. As soon as she was old enough,
Strong enough, Antigone made herself my eyes,
Guiding me, wandering, hungry, barefoot,
Dark woods, sharp rain, spears of the sun.
She could have stayed at home,
A princess in comfort –
And chose to tramp with me.

And you, Ismene, you bring secret messages,
You slip out of Thebes with news.
They banished me and still you cherish me,
You stand by me. What is it?
One loyal slave . . . you slipped away . . .
Important news. What is it?

ISMENE. It wasn't easy, father,
Tracking you, finding you.
To tell it's to live it again. I won't.
I'll tell what's happened.
Your sons, father,
Our brothers, cursed of the gods:

I've news of them.
At first, to rescue Thebes from the family curse,
They gave their throne, their power, to Kreon,
Of their own free will surrendered it.
Then God stole their minds.
Ambition, rivalry, took hold.
Each demanded sole rule, sole power.
Eteokles won, exiled his brother,
His own brother, Polyneikes,
Your heir, the eldest.
Now Polyneikes is in Argos, its ring of hills:
He's raising an army there, they say,
Spear-friends who'll fight till Argos crushes Thebes,
Or die in the dust. No rumours, father: facts.
God treads you down. No pity. He won't let go.

OEDIPUS. You expected that?

ISMENE. Yes, father. The prophet said –

OEDIPUS. Another prophecy!

ISMENE. 'Thebes needs him.
    He'll save them. Alive or dead, they'll need him.'

OEDIPUS. What use am I?

ISMENE. You're strength to them.

OEDIPUS. I'm nothing. I'm dead.

ISMENE. God killed you,
    God gives you life again.

OEDIPUS. I was young, God ended me;
    Now I'm old, I'm to live again?

ISMENE. Kreon's coming.

OEDIPUS. What for?

ISMENE. He needs you near Thebes.
　　Not in it, near. He needs to control you.

OEDIPUS. How can I help my Thebes,
　　From outside the walls?

ISMENE. Unless they give you fair burial,
　　They die.

OEDIPUS. We need no prophets to tell us that.

ISMENE. They want you there, at hand,
　　In their power.

OEDIPUS. They'll bury me in Thebes?

ISMENE. No. You killed your father.

OEDIPUS. In that case, I give them nothing.

ISMENE. It's coming, father,
　　A day of tears for Thebes.

OEDIPUS. What day?

ISMENE. When they stand by your grave,
　　And feel your fury.

OEDIPUS. Who told you this?

ISMENE. They sent to Delphi to ask the oracle.

OEDIPUS. These were Apollo's words?

ISMENE. So they told us.

OEDIPUS. And my sons: do they know this?

ISMENE. They know.

OEDIPUS. They could give back my throne,
And they prefer to keep it? Unendurable!

ISMENE. It's there. Endure it.

OEDIPUS. This I pray for them:
Unceasing war,
War to the death,
No favour from God,
My curse on them.
Both die:
That one who holds my throne,
That other one, exile in Argos,
Die, both die.
They watched their father,
Their begetter, banished.
They could have argued for me,
Helped me; they stood and watched.

What's that? I asked,
I begged my citizens to banish me?
This was my will?
At first, perhaps, that first day,
My heart blazed, I begged them,
My people, to kill me, stone me dead –
And they refused. They let me live.
Heart cooled; I'd asked too much,
Even for what I did, too much –
And then, then it was, they banished me,
Their will, not mine –

And my sons did nothing,
Said nothing, stood and watched me go.
These girls were all I had.
They're all I have.
They feed me, guide me, help me.
Their brothers sold their own father
For power, royal power.

They'll reign without my help,
And they'll not save Thebes.
I know it. Apollo's oracle: I know it.
God sends his truth; he sent us truth before.
I won't help Thebes. Let Kreon beg,
Let them send any lord they like,
I'll not help Thebes.

You, strangers, you and your goddesses,
The Dread Ones, if you stand by me now,
I'll help your city and crush my enemies.

CHORUS. We pity you, Oedipus,
    You and your daughters.
    You offer us help, you say you'll help Athens;
    Listen now, hear what to do.

OEDIPUS. Thankyou. Tell me.

CHORUS. First, purify yourself.
    You walked in their sacred grove,
    The Dread Ones: you must purify yourself.

OEDIPUS. How? Sirs, tell me.

CHORUS. Make offering.
    Clean hands, pure water, the sacred stream.

OEDIPUS. How shall I fetch it?

CHORUS. Cups there you'll find. Fine worksmanship.
　　Bind their lips, their handles.

OEDIPUS. Bind with what?

CHORUS. Lambs' wool, new-shorn.
　　There are priests. They'll help you.

OEDIPUS. And after that?

CHORUS. Face the rising sun, make offering.

OEDIPUS. From the cups?

CHORUS. Three times.
　　One third; one third; the whole.

OEDIPUS. The last one different?

CHORUS. Yes: water and honey mixed. No wine.

OEDIPUS. Dark earth drinks offering. What then?

CHORUS. Three nines of olive twigs.
　　Lay them out – both hands – and pray.

OEDIPUS. What prayer?

CHORUS. That the goddesses,
　　The Kind Ones we call them,
　　May smile on you, hear you,
　　Their suppliant, like them, a saviour.
　　Don't pray aloud, pray silently,
　　Then turn, don't look back, and go.

　　If you make this prayer,
　　Or someone makes it for you,

We'll help you, we won't refuse.
If you don't, my lord, we daren't.

OEDIPUS. Antigone, Ismene – you heard?

ANTIGONE. We heard.

OEDIPUS. I can't go myself.
I'm weak, I'm blind.
One of you must go.
The other, stay and help me.

ISMENE. I'll go. But where?

CHORUS. There, child. Through the trees.
The attendant will show you.

ISMENE. Antigone, stay with father.
He can't be left. He needs us.

Exit. Music.

CHORUS. Old sorrows sleep.
To wake them, cruel.
But still, but still –

OEDIPUS. What is it?

CHORUS. Such agony,
Pain beyond cure –
Tell us, tell us.

OEDIPUS. Kind friends.
Don't make me.

CHORUS. Rumours,
Rumours we've heard.
We ask for truth.

OEDIPUS. Oh moee.

CHORUS. Be patient. Tell.

OEDIPUS. Feoo, feoo.

CHORUS. You asked us to help; we helped.

OEDIPUS. Injustice!
    Done to me! Done to me!
    God knows I was innocent.

CHORUS. What injustice?

OEDIPUS. For my city's sake,
    Married where I should not be married.

CHORUS. To your mother?
    Your mother-wife?

OEDIPUS. Oh moee.
    Death to my ears.
    These children –

CHORUS. Don't say it.

OEDIPUS. My daughters –

CHORUS. Zeus, no!

OEDIPUS. Born of her pain,
    My mother's pain.

CHORUS. Your children.

OEDIPUS. Their father's sisters.

CHORUS. Eeoh.

OEDIPUS. Eeoh, pain on pain.

CHORUS. To suffer so.

OEDIPUS. To suffer so.

CHORUS. You chose it.

OEDIPUS. No.

CHORUS. Not so?

OEDIPUS. They gave her to me.
I saved their city; they gave her.
How could I know?

CHORUS. That blood you shed.

OEDIPUS. No more.

CHORUS. Your father's blood.

OEDIPUS. Papa-ee. Pain piled on pain.

CHORUS. You killed him.

OEDIPUS. Killed him.

CHORUS. For what?

OEDIPUS. For justice.

CHORUS. For justice?

OEDIPUS. He threatened my life;
I killed him. I'm innocent.
I broke no law.

Music ends.

CHORUS. His Majesty's coming.
Theseus son of Aigeus.

You asked for him, to help you.
He's here.

Enter THESEUS.

THESEUS. Oedipus, son of Laios, I knew
About your eyes, what you did to your eyes.
They told me about your rags.
Now I see you. I recognise you. I pity you.
How can we help you? What brings you here,
You and your companion? I'll not refuse.
I too grew up in exile, fought for life abroad.
An exile: I'll do what I can for you. I'm mortal –
Tomorrow I may be in need, like you today.

OEDIPUS. Theseus, kind words, a noble heart.
I'll answer briefly. You know who I am,
My father's name, my country. In a few words
I'll tell why I came, and the story's done.

THESEUS. I'm listening.

OEDIPUS. A gift I bring: myself.
Disfigured; hideous; priceless.

THESEUS. How, priceless?

OEDIPUS. You'll find out, later.

THESEUS. How, later? When?

OEDIPUS. When I leave this world,
And you bury me.

THESEUS. That's all you ask?
The last gift humans give each other?
From now till then – that doesn't worry you?

OEDIPUS. That's all I ask.

THESEUS. Not much.

OEDIPUS. Think carefully.
  It leads to trouble.

THESEUS. Between your sons and me?

OEDIPUS. They want me in Thebes.
  They need me.

THESEUS. And you? Give in, go home:
  When the alternative is exile –

OEDIPUS. I offered it, before. They refused.

THESEUS. And still you're angry?
  A beggar, angry? It's foolish.

OEDIPUS. Foolish? Hear what I say –
  Then if you still think I'm foolish, say so.

THESEUS. I'm sorry. Speak.

OEDIPUS. Theseus, you see a man much wronged.

THESEUS. Your family curse?

OEDIPUS. All Greece knows that.

THESEUS. What else?

OEDIPUS. Banishment.
  At my own sons' hands.
  Forever.
  The father-killer, exiled.

THESEUS. But they wanted you back, you said.

OEDIPUS. God spoke.

THESEUS. An oracle?

OEDIPUS. God prophesied disaster. Here.

THESEUS. Trouble here?
   Between Thebes and Athens?
   Not possible.

OEDIPUS. Lord Theseus, we're mortals.
   We're ruled by Time.
   Only gods live free of it.
   It withers everything:
   Earth's goodness,
   Human strength, good faith.
   Distrust grows rank,
   Friend turns on friend,
   Old allies snap and snarl,
   What we loved we hate,
   We fawn on what we loathed.
   Today blue skies,
   Fair weather between you and Thebes –
   But Time advances,
   Day after day after day,
   And in that time, one speck of time,
   Who knows
   What argument will tear this harmony?
   I'll be cold in the ground.
   I'll gulp warm blood,
   If God is God,
   If oracles speak true.

   No more.

I'll not tell all I know.
Keep your promise, welcome me,
And if God is God, you'll be rewarded.

CHORUS. He means it, Majesty.
It's what he said before.

THESEUS. Who can refuse him –
An old ally, a friend,
Protected by these goddesses?
He offers us blessings.
We've no reason to refuse.
If he stays here, here in this place,
Look after him. Or if he chooses,
He can come with me. Oedipus,
Your choice. It's as you wish.

OEDIPUS. God reward such kindness.

THESEUS. Will you come to the palace?

OEDIPUS. I would have come.
But this is the place –

THESEUS. For what?
Stay here of course, but why?

OEDIPUS. It's here, God said, I'll punish them.

THESEUS. That's the gift you offer us?

OEDIPUS. If you keep your promise.

THESEUS. I give my word.

OEDIPUS. No need for oaths.

THESEUS. As you say: no need for oaths.

OEDIPUS. And if they –

THESEUS. You're afraid – of what?

OEDIPUS. If they come in force – ?

THESEUS. These men are here.

OEDIPUS. If you leave me –

THESEUS. I must.

OEDIPUS. I'm afraid.

THESEUS. No need.

OEDIPUS. But their threats –

THESEUS. Unless I will otherwise, here you stay.
    What are threats? They're gales, they're storms –
    Gone in a puff of smoke, when sense returns.
    They've poured out threats –
    They'll come, they'll snatch –
    Words, not deeds: there's a gulf between.
    You're safe. Apollo sent you,
    You're under my protection.
    You've nothing to fear. You're safe.

Exit. Music.

CHORUS. Chalk-meadows, horses grazing,
    A crown of cottages: Kolonos.
    Dark thickets, a tangle of ivy, laurel.
    Peacefulness.
    Nightingales throbbing, throbbing.
    God walks here:
    In darkness, in stillness,

Dionysos treads.

In morning dew Narcissus bathes,
Yellow crocuses, a crown of flowers
For goddesses,
For great ones. Sleepless,
Springs rustle. Kephisos,
Swelling, feeds our trees.
Here Aphrodite rides,
Here Muses dance.

Here olives grow,
Grey leaves, immortal,
Protected by the gods:
Our gift, our privilege
From Zeus, grey-eyed Athene,
Ours.

Here horses thrive,
Ships, Poseidon's gifts.
We harness them, we ride,
We feather the ocean,
White horses galloping,
Dancing.

Dance. Music ends. Then:

ANTIGONE. A lovely place. Proud words.
Now match them, match them!

OEDIPUS. What is it?

ANTIGONE. Kreon's here, with soldiers.

OEDIPUS. Friends, help me.
It's happening. I need you.

CHORUS. You're safe. We're old,
　　But our country's young, and strong.

Enter KREON, *attended*.

KREON. Villagers. Gentlemen.
　　You look alarmed.
　　There's nothing to fear,
　　No need for defiance:
　　I'm an old man: look.
　　And I know your country's power –
　　The greatest in Greece. I mean no harm.
　　I've come to persuade him back to Thebes.
　　His people sent me, the people of Thebes:
　　I bear their words. They chose me, sent me.
　　Close kin –
　　Who feels his suffering as much as I?

　　Unhappy Oedipus. Come home with me.
　　Do it. I'm on my knees,
　　Your people are on their knees.
　　Trust me. Why should I lie to you?
　　I'm full of tears, look.
　　You're old, you're sick, in exile,
　　Your attendant one little girl,
　　Begging. She wasn't born for this!
　　She should be married, look at her,
　　Trudging after you, drudging, easy prey.

　　Your shame, lord.
　　My shame, our family's shame:
　　It can't be hidden. End it.
　　Wipe it away, come home.
　　Say goodbye to this place, these friends.

You owe it to Thebes, your Thebes. Come home.

OEDIPUS. How dare you?
Snares, nets of words.
I slipped away,
And now you'll drag me back.
When I was sick before,
After what I did,
When I cried and cried for exile,
You refused it –
And as soon as I was calm, accepting,
You threw me out.
Close kin, you say –
What claims had kinship then?
I'm welcome here, they want me;
You paste on smiles to woo me home.

I know what you want.
I know what lurks.
I won't have it.
You beg and beg – and nothing;
Then when you want no more,
They offer it –
Would you accept such charity?

I'll explain to them,
What you say and what you mean.
You want me home, you say. You don't.
You want to plant me on your borders,
A talisman, protection against invasion,
A guarantee. It's denied. Instead
I give you my curse.
I curse the soil of Thebes,

I curse my sons,
Their inheritance,
The graves they'll lie in.
I speak Apollo's words,
God's words, your future.

You've honed your tongue –
Clever words, razors of words –
You've failed.
You thought you'd save Thebes –
You won't.
You don't believe me?
Go home. We stay.
We prefer our pain,
We glory in our pain.

KREON. You've made up your mind.
    You hurt yourself, not me.

OEDIPUS. You've wasted your words –
    On me, on them. I'm happy.

KREON. You're a fool.
    Age brings no sense.
    You disgrace your age.

OEDIPUS. Keep talking!
    You always keep talking.
    What's the point of talking?

KREON. None, if it's nonsense.

OEDIPUS. You condemn yourself.

KREON. Whatever you say.

OEDIPUS. Out! Go home!
  I speak for these men.
  Stop threatening me, nannying me –
  I'm staying.

KREON. Friends, hear him.
  You heard how I spoke to him,
  How he answers me. If once
  I have him home –

OEDIPUS. Oh, look at them. You won't.

KREON. You'll regret this.

OEDIPUS. How, how, my lord?

KREON. Your daughters.
  I've arrested one: she's gone.
  They're fetching the other now.

OEDIPUS. Oee moee.

KREON. I said you'd regret it.

OEDIPUS. My daughter, gone.

KREON. Soon, both.

OEDIPUS. Friends! See what he does.
  You promised.

CHORUS. You. Out of here.
  Respect this place.

KREON (*to the* SOLDIERS). Take her.
  If necessary, by force.

ANTIGONE. Oee moee.

Help me. Gods, mortals, help me.

CHORUS. How dare you?

KREON. What's the matter?
I'm not touching him.

OEDIPUS. My friends –

CHORUS. An outrage.

KREON. She's mine.

CHORUS. How yours?

KREON. My niece. My property.

Music.

OEDIPUS. Eeoh Athens!

CHORUS. Let her go. We'll make you.

KREON. Stand back.

CHORUS. You'll suffer.

KREON. One touch, it's war.

OEDIPUS. I said so.

CHORUS. Hands off her, now!

KREON. You're powerless.

CHORUS. Let her go.

KREON. Get out of the way.

CHORUS. Help!
He's attacking us.

Help us! Help!

Music ends. The SOLDIERS *have pinioned* ANTIGONE.

ANTIGONE. Help me! Friends.

OEDIPUS. Where are you, child?

ANTIGONE. Rape!

OEDIPUS. Give me your hand.

ANTIGONE. I can't.

KREON. Take her. Hurry.

The SOLDIERS *remove* ANTIGONE.

OEDIPUS. What can I do?

KREON. You used them as props. No more.
   They're gone. As for that other thing:
   You refuse to help your country,
   Your people who sent me. So be it.
   Your fury, lord: it spoiled you before,
   It'll spoil you now. You won't take help,
   Won't take advice. You destroy yourself.

CHORUS. Stay where you are.

KREON. Out of the way.

CHORUS. Let them go.

KREON. I'll take another hostage.

CHORUS. What d'you mean?

KREON. This one.

CHORUS. You can't.

KREON. I do as I like.

CHORUS. His Majesty will stop you.

OEDIPUS. You'd lay hands on me?
  In a sacred place?

KREON. You shut your mouth.

OEDIPUS. Ladies, goddesses, help me! Curse him,
  Help me curse him. He snatched my eyes,
  Antigone, my eyes: may the Sun above
  Who sees all things, the eye of God,
  Treat you as you treat me.

KREON. You see, Athenians?

OEDIPUS. They see what you do. They know
  I've no defence but words.

KREON. I'll not give up. I'm old, I'm alone,
  No guards – but still I'll take you.

  Music, as before.

OEDIPUS. Eeoh, Athens.

CHORUS. Stranger. How dare you?

KREON. I dare it.

CHORUS. You break the law.

KREON. In Justice's name.

OEDIPUS. Blasphemy.

CHORUS. You'll fail.

KREON. Zeus judge me.

CHORUS. Sacrilege!

KREON. You can't escape.

CHORUS. Help!
  He's attacking us.
  Help! Oh help!

Music ends. Enter THESEUS, *attended.*

THESEUS. Who's shouting? What's happening?
  I was praying to Poseidon,
  Our protector, horselord –
  This noise interrupted.
  I broke off my prayer,
  I hurried here. What is it?

OEDIPUS. Dear voice. I know you.
  Help me. Sacrilege. He's hurting me.

THESEUS. Who's hurting you?

OEDIPUS. Kreon. That man there.
  He stole my child.

THESEUS. Stole her?

OEDIPUS. She was all I had.

THESEUS. One of you, run to the altar. Guards,
  Send guards to the crossroads. At once.
  Men-at-arms, horsemen, full gallop.
  They must rescue those girls, arrest
  Their kidnappers. I won't be challenged.

  As for this one here: if I dealt with him

As he deserves, he'd feel my fury.
Force, lord: you brought it, now feel it.
You'll stay where you are till those girls are found.
You trample our laws, insult our state,
Snatch anyone you please.
D'you think we're nobodies,
A city of nobodies, unmanned, unkinged?
Thebes never taught you this –
A civilised place, the rule of law.
Kidnapping, insolence, blasphemy:
They'd not find praise in Thebes.
I'd not do this, rampage through your streets,
Barnstorm your holy places, rape citizens,
Justified or not, without permission.
I'd remember my place, your Honour:
A visitor, a stranger, I'd ask before I acted.

So be it. You're old, you're foolish –
It's hardly Thebes' fault. But hear and obey:
I say it again: give back those girls, at once,
Or else enjoy our hospitality. I mean it.

CHORUS. There, stranger.
    There's right and wrong in this –
    And you chose wrong.

KREON. A city of nobodies?
    No, Majesty. Theseus, Aigeus' son.
    I never imagined such a place would take
    A kinsman of mine, would harbour him
    Against my will. Pollution, Majesty.
    He killed his father, mated with his mother –
    You talk of sacrilege! –

He's a tramp, an outcast:
I never thought he'd find friends in Athens,
Never considered it. That's why I claimed him.
Even then, I was for sparing him –
But he heaped such curses on me and mine
That I was left no choice. Due punishment.
I may be old, Majesty, but I have my pride.
Ignore such insults? I'd be dead, my lord.

Well, do what you like. I'm powerless.
In the right, but powerless. Do what you like –
But remember, old men can still fight back.

OEDIPUS. How dare you?
  'Old men can still fight back'!
  You pour it all out – what I did
  To my father, my marriage, my misery,
  My endless misery. How could I know?
  How could I stop? The gods did this,
  Their rage against my house.
  I was innocent. What did I do?
  You'll say I plotted in the dark –
  Well, how was that, exactly?
  How did I plan such things?
  God's oracle said my father's son would kill him –
  How was that my fault?
  I wasn't even born:
  No father yet, no mother,
  I wasn't born. Then later,
  Child of tears, I met a man,
  A stranger, I fought him, killed him –
  My father, how was I to know?

My mother, then – aren't you ashamed
To make me speak of your sister's marriage?
You're not ashamed.
Oh moee moee. You make me speak.
I married my mother, she married her son –
How could we know? She bore my children.
Our shame, your Honour; your pleasure
To talk of it, to make me talk of it.
I did it, I shudder to speak of it,
But still I was innocent. The murder, the marriage,
Shout them as often as you like, I won't be blamed.
Imagine this:
You're an innocent man, a stranger comes
And threatens your life – do you ask him first
If he's your father, or defend yourself?
You wouldn't discuss rights and wrongs,
You'd fight. Well, so did I.

They did it, the gods did this.
If my father came back to life
He'd not deny it. Only you,
Your Honour no Honour,
Persist in denying the truth of it.
You pour out your slander,
You swamp their ears.
Cringe at Theseus' name!
Fawn over Athens!
Haven't you noticed, they respect the gods?
You kidnap my daughters from holy ground,
Under the noses of the gods, you try
To snatch the old man they protect –
I pray to them, ladies, on my knees I pray,

Help me! Punish him! Show him where this is!

CHORUS. He's a good man, Majesty,
Though cursed. He deserves protection.

THESEUS. Enough talk. While we stand talking,
They're on the move, the criminals.

KREON. Say what you want. I'll not resist.

THESEUS. Lead the way. I'm behind you.
If you've hidden those girls in here,
Show me them. If they've gone,
No matter. My men will find them.
None of your soldiers will get back home
To thank their gods. Go on. No choice:
You gambled, and lost. And I tell you this:
You'd accomplices, Athenians.
You'd not have tried this escapade
Without them. And you've lost them. Dead.
I'll see to that. We'll run no risks from you.
D'you hear what I say? Or treat my words
As lightly as the warnings from these old men?

KREON. I won't argue.
At home, we'll know what to do.

THESEUS. Threaten all you like, but march!
Oedipus, stay here. You're safe. Be calm.
I give you my word: I'll bring them back,
Your daughters, or die beside them.

OEDIPUS. God save you, Theseus. Majesty.
God reward you for helping me.

Exeunt THESEUS, KREON *and* SOLDIERS. *Music.*

CHORUS. They're fighting,
Soldiers.
Spears sing,
Blade locks with blade.
There in the shrine,
Holiness, silence,
Golden on praying tongues.
He's there! He's there!
Theseus our Majesty:
Saving them.

They've escaped:
Green fields,
White rocks,
Pelting, pelting.

Ares, warlord,
Athene, Poseidon,
Snatch us there!
Blade lock with blade.
Theseus our Majesty:
Fall on them.

Silence. It's over.
They're rescued.
We've rescued them.
God grant it.
Let me soar, white wings,
A dove, let me see, let me see.

Zeus sees all, rules all.
Guide their hands.
Athene, lady,
Apollo,

Artemis, be near,
Hear and help, we cry to you.

Music ends.

Wanderer, trust me.
They're coming, I see them.
Your daughters, coming.

OEDIPUS. Where? How? Coming?

Enter THESEUS, ANTIGONE, ISMENE *and*
SOLDIERS.

ANTIGONE. Father, O father,
He's rescued us.
God bless him.
If only you'd eyes to see him.

OEDIPUS. Antigone. You're safe.

ANTIGONE. He did it. His dear hands.
Theseus. His soldiers.

OEDIPUS. Come closer. Let me kiss you.
I thought you'd gone forever.

ANTIGONE. You prayed to the gods. They answered.

OEDIPUS. Are you there?

ANTIGONE. Beside you. Both of us.

OEDIPUS. Darlings.

ANTIGONE. Daddy.

OEDIPUS. Helpers.

ANTIGONE. Sharers.

OEDIPUS. Nothing's more to me.
　　Now I could die.
　　Hold me. Hug me.
　　One on each side.
　　I was lost; I'm found again.
　　How did it . . . ? Tell me how it . . .

ANTIGONE. Theseus rescued us, father.
　　He's here, he'll tell you. Ask him.

OEDIPUS. Sir, I'm sorry: an old man's tears.
　　My daughters, I thought they'd gone.
　　They say you rescued them,
　　It's thanks to you, you, Majesty: this joy.
　　God reward you, you and your country,
　　The only place in all the world
　　Where justice lives, where truth is told,
　　Where gods are honoured. It's thanks to you.
　　Give me your hand. May I kiss your cheek?
　　I can't ask that. The man the whole world hates,
　　Humanity's scapegoat – touch you, touch you?
　　My burden. Mine only.
　　Words only. Thankyou.
　　Be kind to me always,
　　As you are today.

THESEUS. You weep to see them:
　　No surprise in that.
　　Your first words for them, not me:
　　Who'll blame you?
　　I did what you asked; I kept my word;
　　I need no thanks.

You ask how it happened, the fight we fought?
They'll tell you. One other thing first.
Advise me. A strange thing, I heard just now,
Coming back: small, but perhaps important.

OEDIPUS. What, Majesty?
We've heard nothing here.

THESEUS. At Poseidon's altar –
Where I was praying just now,
When they called me to help you –
A man's there, sitting, in sanctuary.
No one knows where he came from.
Your relative, they say, but not from Thebes.

OEDIPUS. Where, then? And sanctuary – why?

THESEUS. All I know is, he asks for you:
A few words only, then safe-conduct, out.

OEDIPUS. But why does he need sanctuary?

THESEUS. Who needs to ask your blessing?
Someone, for example, from Argos – ?

OEDIPUS. Argos! Ah.

THESEUS. What is it?

OEDIPUS. No, Majesty.

THESEUS. What d'you mean?

OEDIPUS. Ask no more.

THESEUS. I don't understand.

OEDIPUS. I know who it is.

THESEUS. Who? Why does he ask safe-conduct?

OEDIPUS. My son, Majesty. The hated one,
The one I hate, I'll not receive.

THESEUS. He wants only words:
To be heard, no more.

OEDIPUS. The man I hate: my son.
I won't hear him. He scalds my ears.

THESEUS. He asks in the name of God.

ANTIGONE. Father. Listen. Do it.
Not because I say so: I'm far too young.
For his sake, for his Majesty's sake,
For God. Let him speak to you, our brother.
How can he hurt you? How change your mind?
He can't. If he's plotting, you'll soon know,
What he says will tell you. He's your son:
He's hurt you, wronged you, but see him.
Children harm their parents. He spoke sharp words,
But parents should forgive, should listen.
Remember your father, your mother,
What they did to you,
Your agony that came from what they did –
Remember it, put rage aside. See him,
For my sake, for Ismene's sake.
We're on our knees.
After all we've done for you, do this for us.

OEDIPUS. It hurts me, child. But I'll do it.
Since you ask, I'll do it.
This only, Majesty: if he comes here,
Don't let him touch me.

THESEUS. I gave you my word;
   Again I give it. In round terms, Oedipus:
   As Theseus is safe in the hands of God,
   So you are safe in mine.

   Exit. Music.

CHORUS. Pebbles on a beach,
   Wave-washed, wind-beaten,
   North, West, East, South,
   Storm-thrashed. So Oedipus.

   Ask for life, long life,
   More than mortal term –
   You're a fool. Tears, age, pain,
   Only Death can end them.

   Better not be born.
   Youth skips and laughs,
   Then pains come, anger, blood,
   Old age in ambush, pain.

   Music ends.

ANTIGONE. Someone's coming,
   Alone, in tears,
   Tears streaming down his cheeks.

OEDIPUS. You mean – ?

ANTIGONE. Polyneikes, father.
   It was him they meant. He's here.

   Enter POLYNEIKES.

POLYNEIKES. Antigone! Ismene!
   Things are bad for me –

But for *him*, our father . . . !
Rags. Foul rags.
Hair, wild in the wind.
Stranger with strangers.
No eyes. Food dogs despise.
Now I see. I know.
I should have known before.
I hurt you, father,
I did it, I only, I'm to blame.
But listen. On God's right hand,
Beside God's throne, sits Mercy.
Accept her, father.
What's done is done. It'll heal.
There'll be nothing worse, no more.

Say something.
Father. Don't turn away,
Don't send me away unheard.
You're angry. Tell me why you're angry.
Antigone, Ismene, ask him to speak.
Reach him. Help me. In the name of God.
I come in God's name – ask him to answer.

ANTIGONE. Brother, tell him what you want.
Some word you say may soften him,
Or stoke his fury. In either case, he'll speak.

POLYNEIKES. Good advice.
Poseidon, help me: fill my mouth.
It was at your altar he found me,
Theseus found me, gave me safe-conduct,
Gave me leave to speak, to hear his answer, go.
In God's name, then, strangers, sisters, father –

I'm an exile. Driven from Thebes.
Your eldest son, I claimed your throne,
And Eteokles, young Eteokles, denied me.
No discussion, no argument, exile.
Behind my back, he won Thebes round.
Your Furies, father, still haunt our house:
Apollo's priests confirm it.

I travelled to Argos,
I married Adrastos' daughter,
Made allies, spear-friends,
Of all the warriors there,
It's a land of fighters.
Seven warlords,
Seven armies, like seven sharp spears
Aimed straight at the heart of Thebes.
We swore an oath: die nobly,
Or drive that pretender out. It's decided.

I ask your blessing, father –
For me, for them, the Seven,
That sheaf of spears:
Amphiaraos, prophet and warrior;
Tydeus; Etyoklos; Hippomedon;
Kapaneus, firelord; Parthenopaios sixth,
And last your son, no-son,
Your child of fate, their general.

We're on our knees, father.
We ask your blessing.
For your daughters' sake,
For your own dear life, give up this anger,
Help us. We want to bring him down,

That brother of mine who banished me,
Who stole my Thebes.

We have oracles, father.
We have God's word:
The army you bless will win.
For the sake of Thebes,
Its river-springs, its gods,
Bless me.
We're exiles, beggars, both of us.
We live by smiling at strangers;
Eteokles lords it in our palace,
Lords it and laughs at us.
If you bless me, I'll scatter him,
I'll bring you home, I'll save us both.
If you bless me not, I'm dead.

CHORUS. Oedipus.
For his Majesty, for Theseus
Who sent him here, say something,
Answer.

OEDIPUS. For his Majesty, then,
For Theseus who sent him here,.
I'll unlock my lips.

Blessing, he asks. Denied.

Liar!
You had the throne, before he took it,
You had my throne and banished me.
You made me this.
You weep at the rags you gave me,
You taste it yourself, and weep.

No time for tears now, Oedipus.
Hard now, hard always now, remembering.

You did this: yoked me –
The beggar, the sad one,
With none but these to help me.
Daughters. My daughters.
They saved their father.
I have no sons.

God's watching you.
The eye of Fate is on you.
Your armies swarm on Thebes:
They'll die, you'll die,
You won't take Thebes.
You'll smother in his blood,
Your brother's blood,
You'll drown in it.
He'll die in yours.

I curse you. Both.
I cursed you then, I curse you now.
My words are knives.
I call my Furies, my spear-friends,
Down on you. Learn this:
You should have honoured your father,
The blind one, respected him
As my daughters did; you didn't.
Learn this, and die for it.
You're on your knees,
You claim your throne?
In Justice's name,
Who sits with Zeus above,
I spit on you.

Out.
Who wants you? You're dead.
I disown you. Curse you.
Go.
Never win back Thebes,
Never hide in Argos,
Die at your brother's hand,
Kill him, and die.
Gods of the Underworld,
Furies who guard these trees,
Ares, wargod, hear these prayers.
You, go.
Tell Thebes, tell your friends,
Your spear-friends,
How Oedipus has blessed his sons.

CHORUS. Polyneikes, go now.
　　You walk in wickedness. Go, go.

POLYNEIKES. Why did I do this –
　　Make allies, set out from Argos?
　　How can I tell them – tell this?
　　There's no turning back. I must,
　　The future's fixed, I must.
　　Antigone, Ismene, since this is so,
　　Since what our father says is so,
　　If you ever come home, come to Thebes,
　　Our Thebes, remember me.
　　Don't hurt me more. Be kind.
　　Bury me, respect me.
　　He praises you; I'll praise you too,
　　The whole world will judge what you do for me.

ANTIGONE. Polyneikes, please –

POLYNEIKES. I'm listening.

ANTIGONE. Order them home, the army.
    Don't kill our Thebes; don't die.

POLYNEIKES. They're marching.
    If I flinch from this, I'm finished.

ANTIGONE. And for this, for this,
    You'll sack our Thebes?

POLYNEIKES. What else am I to do?
    Let Eteokles rule? Let him laugh at me?
    Run into exile and let him laugh?

ANTIGONE. You'll die. Both die.
    Father said so.

POLYNEIKES. We'll obey his wishes.

ANTIGONE. Oee moee. Who'll follow you?
    When they hear this curse, and follow you?

POLYNEIKES. No curse they'll hear from me.
    Why scare them away? Why tell it?
    Wise generals keep their counsel.

ANTIGONE. You won't give way?

POLYNEIKES. Don't waste your words.
    Darkness, Furies, our father –
    My path is set.
    God smile on you, sisters,
    God send you happiness,

Let you give me the gift I beg,
Last gift, on the day I die.

It's time. Goodbye.

ANTIGONE. Darling –

POLYNEIKES. Don't cry.

ANTIGONE. You slip away,
Slip into darkness –
Oh let me weep.

POLYNEIKES. I accept my fate.

ANTIGONE. You needn't.

POLYNEIKES. I must.

ANTIGONE. How can I live without you?

POLYNEIKES. It's in God's hands.
Antigone, Ismene,
You're in God's hands.
Be happy. You've earned it.
God end this pain.

Exit. Music.

CHORUS. It swoops.
Blind eyes,
Dark words,
Evil swoops.
God chooses,
Fate.

Thunder!
All heaven shakes.

Time lifts us up,
Casts down.
It's now,
It's now.

Music ends.

OEDIPUS. Children, it's happening.
It's now, Fate's now.
Send someone for Theseus.

ANTIGONE. What's happening?

OEDIPUS. Thunder-wings.
God's words.
Earth gapes, Dark calls me.
Fetch Theseus. Fetch him.

Music.

CHORUS. It falls,
It roars,
Sears sky:
Lightning,
God's lightning,.
Now.

It's now,
It's happening:
Greatness, happening.
We see,
We cower,
It's now.

Music ends.

OEDIPUS. God calls me.
  Children, no escape.

ANTIGONE. Father, how can you tell?

OEDIPUS. It's coming.
  I see it. Fetch his Majesty.

  Music.

CHORUS. Eeah eeah.
  Again,
  It roars,
  It flares.
  Help us,
  God above,
  Zeus above,
  We cry.

  Music ends.

OEDIPUS. Is he here?
  Can you see him?
  All's dark.
  Hurry him, hurry him.

ANTIGONE. Why, father, why?

OEDIPUS. Blessing.
  I promised.
  Blessing.
  I'll do it.

  Music.

CHORUS. Eeoh eeoh.
  Come, lord,

Hurry,
Help us,
Leave it,
God's altar,
Hurry, lord,
Hurry.

Music ends. Enter THESEUS.

THESEUS. More shouting:
The stranger, my people.
Thunder, lightning,
All heaven in uproar –
What is it?

OEDIPUS. Majesty, you're here.
God be thanked,
God bless you.

THESEUS. Son of Laios, what is it?

OEDIPUS. My life winds down. It's time.
The blessing I promised.

THESEUS. It's time. How can you tell?

OEDIPUS. God calls me. Signs and portents –

THESEUS. Explain.

OEDIPUS. Thunder, lightning. His mighty hand.

THESEUS. I accept what you say. What must I do?

OEDIPUS. Majesty, I tell a secret.
Store it, keep it,
A blessing for your city forever.

Take my hand. I'll lead you –
No guides, no companions –
To where my life will end.
Tell no one. Show no one. Ever.
Till the end of time, that place will be
A protection
More than a thousand shields,
Ten thousand allies.
You'll see a mystery.
No one must know, save you alone –
Not these citizens,
Not (alas) my daughters.
Lock it in your heart.
When your own death nears
Tell one person only:
Your chosen one.
Let him do the same,
His chosen one the same,
Forever.
Do this, keep your city safe,
From the dragon-seed of Thebes,
From the myriad arguments
That flare between state and state.

We think we live justly,
But God's on watch,
God notices,
Sees how we trample justice,
Trample honour,
In the madness of our hearts –
Sees and punishes.
Majesty, avoid it!

I've said enough. You understand.
It's time. God's ready, guiding me.
Give me your hand.
Little ones, come after.
Keep your distance.
You led me once; I lead you now.
Don't touch me:
I'll find it, my resting-place,
Chosen by God.
This way. This way.
They're calling me,
Persephone queen of the Underworld,
Hermes, soul-guide.

Sunlight!
How long since I saw you last.
Now I feel you, I bathe in you . . .

No more. It's over.
Lie down, forever, sleep.
Majesty, my blessing – on you,
Your land, your people.
You befriended me. Be blessed,
And in your blessedness,
Remember me.

Music. Exeunt all but CHORUS.

CHORUS. Humbly we pray.
    Ladies, be gracious.
    Hades, Hades,
    Grant him quietness,
    Passing without pain

As he journeys
To silence, darkness,
His suffering done.
He deserves it; grant it.

Spirits of Hell,
Grim guardian
Howling, howling
In vaults of dark,
Let him pass in peace.
Lull him asleep,
Sing lullabies,
Enfold him.
Peace now, unending rest.

Dance. Music ends. Enter SOLDIER.

SOLDIER. Athenians. Few words.
   Lord Oedipus' life is done.
   I'll tell what I saw.

CHORUS. Found peace at last.

SOLDIER. Slipped free at last.

CHORUS. Did God do this? Tell what you saw.

SOLDIER. It was wonderful. You saw him go,
   Unhelped, leading the way for us.
   He went as far as the Entrance,
   Bronze Floor, the plunge into Hell.
   The crossroad's there, the hollow
   Where Theseus and Pirithous slew cattle
   Years ago, brink of the Underworld.
   Thorikos' Cliff; wild fig; stone monument.

He sat, stripped off his rags,
Asked his daughters to fetch water
For washing, for offering.
They went to Demeter's Hill, Leaf-lady,
Fetched water, washed him,
Dressed him as we dress the dead.

They finished. He was satisfied.
A peal of thunder, underground.
The girls shivered, beat their breasts,
Began screaming, sobbing.
He hugged them.
'Little ones, today it must end,
Your father's life.
I'll be no more.
Your burden ends. Hard –
Just one thing eased it: love.
You loved me, I loved you,
More than all the world.
Now we must part.
We must go our ways.'

They held each other, wept.
They stopped.
Silence.
A voice, calling:
'Oedipus! Oedipus!'
God's voice.
Our hair stood on end.
'Come, Oedipus. It's now.'
He called to Theseus, his Majesty,
Put the children's hands in his,
Asked him never to abandon them,

To look after them, always.
His Majesty promised.
Solemnly. No tears.
Then Oedipus felt for the girls again.
'Go now. Be brave.
You mustn't stay, mustn't see.
Only Theseus must see.'

We were all weeping.
We took the girls, aside.
And when we looked back, he'd gone.
His Majesty was there, alone,
Shielding his eyes,
As if he'd seen a sight
No mortal ever sees.
He was praying:
To gods above, below, one prayer.

How Oedipus left the world,
We don't know,
Only Theseus knows.
No fire from Zeus,
No surge of sea –
God's messenger, perhaps,
Earth's portals opening,
Gently, gently,
No pain, no suffering.
A miracle.

You think I dreamt it?
As you wish.
I tell what I saw.

CHORUS. Where are they –
     The girls, the others?

SOLDIER. Coming.
     Listen: tears. They're here.

Music. Enter ANTIGONE *and* ISMENE.

ANTIGONE. Aee aee, feoo.
     Nothing,
     We've nothing,
     All's gone.
     Tears,
     Our destiny.
     While he lived,
     Hard pain.
     Now he's gone,
     God's taken him.

CHORUS. What happened?

ANTIGONE. Who can tell?

CHORUS. He died?

ANTIGONE. No sickness,
     No wound,
     No drowning.
     Secretly,
     Silently.
     He slipped away.
     What's left for us?
     What country,
     What angry sea?
     All's dark for us.

ISMENE. God take me,
  Snatch me down to death,
  Let me die with him.
  What's left for me now?
  I'm alive; I'm dead.

CHORUS. Accept it.
  You were good to him.
  Don't scald yourselves.
  You were good to him.

ANTIGONE. I hold out my arms:
  That old misery,
  That pain, I want it,
  I long for it.
  Father, darling,
  I held you. I weep for you,
  Dead in a foreign land.
  Where are you now?
  How can I hold you now?

CHORUS. It's over.

ANTIGONE. He chose it.

CHORUS. Chose it?

ANTIGONE. This place, this earth:
  He chose it, he lies in it.
  Weep for him, here.
  You've gone, you left us:
  No more for us, you chose it.

ISMENE. Antigone,
  What's left for us?

Where can we go?
How can we live?
He's gone.

CHORUS. An easy death:
His death was easy.
All mortals die.
Be easy.

ANTIGONE. Ismene,
Come with me.

ISMENE. Where?

ANTIGONE. There.
I want it.

ISMENE. He told us, no.

ANTIGONE. Where he lies –
We'll see where he lies.

ISMENE. You mustn't.

ANTIGONE. Don't stop me.

ISMENE. Don't you understand?

ANTIGONE. Tell me.

ISMENE. He had to die alone.
He has no grave.

ANTIGONE. Take me there.
I'll die there too.

ISMENE. Aee aee, and if I do
Who'll care for me?
Who'll care for me?

CHORUS. Children, be easy.

ANTIGONE. Where's safe?

CHORUS. Here's safe.

ANTIGONE. Tell me.

CHORUS. No harm is here.

ANTIGONE. I know it.

CHORUS. Then what – ?

ANTIGONE. What home have we?

CHORUS. It's over.

ANTIGONE. We're lost.

CHORUS. The worst is past.

ANTIGONE. More's coming.

CHORUS. Wave on wave of pain.

ANTIGONE. Feoo feoo.
    Zeus, guide us!
    Where can we go?
    Where's hope for us?

Music ends. Enter THESEUS.

THESEUS. Children, be easy.
    Night cradles him.
    God ordered it:
    No tears.

ANTIGONE. Your Majesty, on our knees –

THESEUS. What is it?

ANTIGONE. Show us where he sleeps.

THESEUS. It's forbidden.

ANTIGONE. You're his Majesty. You can.

THESEUS. No living soul must tread that ground,
　　No living voice be heard: his words.
　　If we obey, he'll bless this land.
　　I promised; God heard; it's done.

ANTIGONE. Then send us home,
　　Send us to Thebes.
　　Blood flows, our brothers are drowning.
　　We'll save them.

THESEUS. I'll do it.
　　Your wishes; his,
　　Who sleeps below –
　　I'll do it.

CHORUS. No tears.
　　It's over.
　　This promise stands.

　　Exeunt.

Glossary and Pronunciation Guide

NB stressed syllable in capitals

ADRASTOS (ad-RASS-toss). King of Argos.

AGENOR (a-GAY-nohr). Legendary ancestor of Laios.

AIGEUS (AIG-yooss, Greek e-YEFS). Mythical king of
Athens, father of Theseus.

AMPHIARAOS: see Seven Against Thebes

ANTIGONE (an-TIG-o-nee, Greek an-ti-GON-ee).
Oedipus' elder daughter.

APHRODITE (af-ro-DIE-tee). Goddess of beauty and desire.

APOLLO (a-POL-lo). God of prophecy.

ARES (AH-rees). God of war.

ARGOS. Warlike city in Southern Greece, once ruled by
Agamemnon.

ARTEMIS (AR-tem-iss). Archer-goddess, Apollo's twin.

ATHENE (ath-EE-nee). Goddess of wisdom.

BACCHOS (BAK-koss). Cult name for Dionysos, patron
god of Thebes.

DAULIA (DO(R)-li-a, Greek dav-LEE-a). Country town
near Thebes.

DELPHI. Apollo's prophetic shrine on Mount Parnassos, regarded as infallible.

DEMETER (dee-MEE-ter). Goddess of harvest, associated with the Underworld because her daughter, Persephone, was its queen.

DIONYSOS (die-on-IE-soss, Greek dee-ON-i-soss). Patron god of Thebes.

ETEOKLES (et-EE-o-klees, Greek e-tee-o-KLEES). Oedipus' younger son.

ETYOKLOS: see Seven Against Thebes.

FURIES. Daughters of Night, Underworld demons who punished those mortals who killed relatives. They were known as Dread Ones, All-seeing Ones, Kind Ones (in Greek, Eumenides) – anything to avoid speaking their real name. The Athenians believed that they also lived in Athens itself, in sacred caves and woods.

HADES (HAY-dees). (1) God of the Underworld. (2) The Underworld.

HERMES (HER-mees). Messenger-god.

HIPPOMEDON: see Seven Against Thebes.

ISMENE (is-MEE-nee). Oedipus' younger daughter.

JOKASTA (yo-KASS-ta). Oedipus' mother and queen.

KADMOS (KAD-moss). Legendary founder of Thebes.

KAPANEUS: see Seven Against Thebes.

KIND ONES: see Furies.

KISTHENE (kiss-THEE-nee). Shrine of Hermes.

KOLONOS (kol-OH-noss). (1) Hero from Athenian legend. (2) Village named after him.

KREON (KREE-on, Greek kre-OHN). Brother of Jokasta. The word is not a personal name, but a title, similar to Egyptian 'pharaoh'. It means 'Powerful'.

LABDAKOS (LAB-da-koss). Father of Laios.

LAIOS (LIE-oss). Oedipus' father. He offended the gods (first by a homosexual liaison, which was forbidden to mortals, and then by murder), and was punished by being informed by the oracle that his own son would murder him.

MENOIKEUS (men-OIK-yoos). Father of Kreon.

MEROPE (me-ROH-pee). Polybos' queen.

OEDIPUS (EE-di-puss, Greek e-DEE-pooss, 'swell-foot'). Son of Laios and Jocasta.

OLYMPIA. Main shrine of Zeus, in southern Greece.

PARTHENOPAIOS: see Seven Against Thebes.

PHOKIS (FOH-kiss). Region between Thebes and Delphi.

PIRITHOUS (pi-RI-tho-uss, Greek pi-ri-THOH-oss). Hero-companion of Theseus who went to the Underworld with him to steal a wife.

POLYBOS (POL-i-boss). Aged ruler of Corinth.

POLYDOROS (pol-li-DOH-ross). Legendary ancestor of Laios.

POLYNEIKES (pol-i-NAY-kees). Oedipus' elder son.

POSEIDON (poss-AY-don). God of the sea and of horses. Thought to be a particular benefactor of Athens.

PROMETHEUS (pro-MEETH-yooss). Titan (supernatural power from the beginning of time, a survivor in the age of the gods). He created humans from mud-dolls, and gave them the gods' fire, which gave them intelligence.

SEVEN AGAINST THEBES. Seven champions who took armies to attack the seven gates of Thebes and win back Polyneikes' kingdom after he was exiled by Eteokles. They were Polyneikes himself, Adrastos, Etyoklos (et-YOK-loss), Hippomedon (hip-OM-e-dohn), Kapaneus (KAP-an-yooss), Parthenopaios (par-then-o-PIE-oss) and Tydeus (TIED-yooss).

SPHINX. A winged lion. It asked the riddle 'What has four legs in the morning, two at noon and three in the evening?', and each day the Thebans failed to find the answer ('A human being') it ate their children.

THESEUS (THEESS-yoos, Greek thee-SEFS). Legendary king of Athens, a hero and friend of Herakles.

TEIRESIAS (tie-REE-si-ass; Greek ter-e-SEE-ass). Blind Theban prophet, infallible and respected, but seldom believed.

THORIKOS' CLIFF (tho-REEK-oss). Rocky outcrop near Athens, a cave in which was one of the entrances to the Underworld.

TYDEUS: see Seven Against Thebes.

ZEUS (NB one syllable only, z-YOOSS, not 'ZOOS'). Supreme god.